the Ultimate Little FROZEN DRINKS BOOK

Ray Foley

SOURCEBOOKS, INC.®
NAPERVILLE, ILLINOIS

Published by Sourcebooks, Inc.
P.O. Box 4410, Naperville, Illinois 60567-4410
(630) 961-3900
FAX: (630) 961-2168
www.sourcebooks.com

Originally published in 2001

Library of Congress Cataloging-in-Publication Data
Foley, Ray.
  Ultimate little frozen drinks book / Ray Foley.
     p. cm.
  ISBN-13: 978-1-4022-0679-5
  ISBN-10: 1-4022-0679-8
  1. Cocktails. 2. Alcoholic beverages. 3. Blenders (Cookery) I. Title.

TX951.F5949 2006
641.8'74—dc22

2005025116

Printed and bound in Canada.
WC 10 9 8 7 6 5 4 3 2 1

DEDICATION

This book is dedicated to all the blender drinkers and bartenders who stir, shake, and serve. Also to Jaclyn Marie and Ryan Foley and the rest of the tribe!

ACKNOWLEDGMENTS

Allied Domecq Spirits USA—Robert Suffredini

Angostura International Ltd.

Austin, Nichols & Co., Inc.

Bacardi USA, Inc.

Banta Book Group—Bob Christopher

Barton Incorporated

Branca Products Corporation

Brown-Forman Beverages Worldwide

Cairns & Associates, Inc.

Charles Jacquin et Cie., Inc.—Patricia Bornmann, John Cooper, Kevin O'Brien

Coco Lopez, Inc.—Jose Suarez, R. Jake Jacobsen

Crillon Importers—Michel Roux, Jerry Ciraulo

Dozortsev & Sons Enterprises, Ltd.

Dunwoodie Communications—Greg Cohen

Heaven Hill Distilleries, Inc.

Jim Beam Brands Worldwide, Inc.

Kobrand Corp.

Kratz & Jensen, Inc.—Christine Deussen, Alicia DiFolco

Major Peters' Bloody Mary mix

Manitowoc Ice, Inc.—Larry Hagman

Marie Brizard Wines and Spirits, USA

Mott's USA—Jeff Polisoto

National Cherry Board—Cheryl Kroupa

Niche Marketing

Rémy Amerique

Schieffelin & Somerset—Jeff Pogash

Seagram North America—Robert Dubin, Arthur Shapiro

Skyy Spirits LLC

Steve Baron Communications

The Baddish Group

The Food Group—Mark Bloom

The Gang at Maker's Mark

Todhunter International, Inc.

Top Shelf Marketing—George and
 Kelly Borrello
UDV North America
Vita Mix
Waring Products—Joan Gioiella

Special thanks to Jimmy Zazzali, Matt
Wojciak, John Cowan, Michael
Cammarano, Charles Chop, Marvin
Solomon, the Rinaldis (Millie and
Anthony), as well as Loretta Natiello and
Erica DeWitte for putting this to paper.
  In addition, to all those who submitted
recipes to www.bartender.com and the
readers of *Bartender* magazine.

Introduction

All recipes have been alphabetized for your convenience.

Techniques of Mixing

1. Blend—All, yes all, cocktails are to be blended with ice. Therefore, all instructions may not read "blend" at the end of each recipe.

2. Glasses—You should use your imagination on choice of glassware. This will add your personal signature to each cocktail. Any type of drinking vessel is permitted. Let your creativity pour wild.

3. Ingredients—Please only use the BEST ingredients—the top of the line. You would not buy cheap meat when cooking a steak. Use top brands—they make top cocktails.

4. Have Fun!

Publisher's Note: This book and the recipes contained herein are intended for those of a legal drinking age. Please drink responsibly and ensure you and your guests have a designated driver when consuming alcoholic beverages.

Short History of the Blender

Waring, universally known for introducing the first blender to American consumers, is one of today's leading manufacturers of professional quality, small appliances for the home, foodservice, and laboratory industries. The company was acquired on May 9, 1998, by Conair Corporation, which also owns Cuisinart.

Although the company is named after Fred Waring, a popular entertainer of the 1930s, 40s, and 50s, Warding did not actually invent the blender. He did, however, perfect the original version and introduce this version to retailers and consumers—which ultimately became a big success. Waring history has it that in 1936, Fred Waring had just finished a radio broadcast in New York's Vanderbilt Theater when Fred Osius, dressed in outlandish striped pants, a cutaway coat, and a bright lemon-yellow tie, approached the entertainer with his latest invention. Osius was looking for someone to finance a new mixer that would "revolutionize people's eating habits."

Waring was intrigued with the concept of a mixer such as the one Osius described, and he agreed to back the new product, even when the prototype failed to work the first time. Six months and $25,000 later, the prototype still didn't work. However, Waring remained enthusiastic and with his support the engineering and production problems were solved in time to introduce the new "Miracle Mixer" (as it was then called) at the National Restaurant Show in Chicago in 1937.

Thanks to Waring's own promotion of the blender on the radio and through a singing group aptly named "The Waring Blendors," the blender became a permanent fixture in restaurants and bars. It wasn't long before consumers decided that they needed blenders in their kitchens as well. Ultimately, department-

and specialty-store sales increased, and the blender became a household appliance for home chefs.

World War II temporarily halted blender production, but in 1946, sales took off again as consumer demand grew. Product innovations continued, with the introduction of color-coordinated blenders and attachments that crushed ice and ground coffee. Solid state controls were among the most significant product changes. In the 1950s, new uses for the blender were constantly emerging, including applications in research laboratories. In fact, Dr. Jonas Salk used a Waring blender with an Aseptic Dispersal Container attachment to develop his life-saving polio vaccine.

During the late 1960s, design and engineering breakthroughs by Waring led to the creation of a more versatile blender that was more efficient and widely affordable. While maintaining its leadership in the blender market, Waring capitalized on its strong brand recognition and expanded its product line with a broad range of fine-quality kitchen appliances.

Fred Waring died in 1984, but his vision for a top quality blender lives on as Waring continues to manufacture an innovative line of top-performance blenders for the home and for commercial use.

Hamilton Beach Commercial Blender Tips

1. Make sure you purchase the right blender for your application.

- Frozen drinks without alcohol require a blender with a more powerful motor.
- Determine the container size based on the maximum drink size and maximum number of drinks that will be blended at one time.
- Stainless steel vs. plastic container is a personal preference, but there's more "show" and ease of loading with plastic and better insulation with stainless steel.
- Blenders with timers allow other tasks to be performed while blending.
- Programmed-cycle blenders provide optimum blend performance.

2. Use ice cubes that have a fewer number of air pockets or smaller cube size for ease in blending.

3. Add liquid ingredients first.

4. Measure ice with the glass the drink will be served in.

5. Ice should be added until it fills to the top of the liquid.

6. If ice cream is in the recipe, it should be added last.

7. Wait until the blade stops rotating before removing the lid.

8. Make sure the blender is off before removing or installing a container.

9. Check the clutch for wear, and replace as needed. (Removes easily per instruction card.)

10. Check the blade assembly periodically, and replace on a regular basis.

Vita-Mix's Top Ten Tips for Blending Liquids

1. Secure the container cover tightly before turning the blender on.

2. Do not place fingers or other objects, such as spoons or spatulas, in the blender container while the motor is running.

3. Do not remove the container cover while processing liquids.

4. If adding beer to a drink, stir it in last. Do not place beer in a blender and then turn it on.

5. When making ice cream drinks, in general, use soft ice cream and add it to the container last. With a Vita-Mix blender, however, you can add hard-packed ice cream or frozen yogurt at any point.

6. For single-serve drinks, add ice first. Pulse ice once or twice. Then add the wet ingredients.

7. When mixing drinks, switch to a higher speed if the motor seems to be laboring.

8. Always unplug the machine before cleaning it.

9. To clean a blender container, fill it halfway with water. Add a few drops of dishwashing detergent. Turn the motor on and blend for a few seconds. Empty the container and rinse it.

10. Keep the machine clean. Store it on a clean surface. Clean the vents regularly.

The History of Coco Lopez

Once upon a Time There Was No Piña Colada...

The heart of the coconut has long been an important ingredient of many delicious desserts in the tropical islands, but getting the coconut cream from the pulp was a task in itself.

Don Ramon

There had to be an easier way, and one man set out to find it. In his small laboratory in Puerto Rico, Don Ramon Lopez Irizarry developed the original Coco Lopez, a delicious homogenized cream made from the tender meat of sun-ripened Caribbean coconuts and blended with the exact proportion of natural cane sugar.

There is only one right moment and way to blend the basic ingredients that make up the original Coco Lopez cream of coconut. And this magical moment always took place in Don Ramon's kitchen.

Limited Production

Success came too suddenly for Don Ramon Lopez Irizarry. His production facilities were limited to his personal efforts. This is when Industrias La Famosa, Puerto Rico's largest processors of canned products, and Don Ramon agreed on mutual goals. The fusion became a transcendental success! After his agreement with Industrias La Famosa, he limited the secret of his expertise to be shared by only two of its stockholders. This unique product was granted with U.S. Patent #2426834.

Recipes Made Easy

Getting the cream from the coconut for desserts and other native dishes was a tedious and laborious task. Coco Lopez made it easy. For this it is preferred by homemakers and has earned its place in the kitchens of the best restaurants and hotels in Puerto Rico.

The Flavorful Piña Colada

Suddenly, Coco Lopez became the basis for a fabulous tropical drink called Piña Colada (pronounced: pee-nyah coh-lah-dah) that made its appearance back in 1967.

Quite a few bartenders and part-time mixers (one at Barra China in Old San Juan, and the other at the Caribe Hilton Hotel in San Juan) claim to be the inventors of the "Official Beverage of Puerto Rico," as proclaimed by the tourism department of Puerto Rico. But there's no doubt that the unique combination of Coco Lopez cream of coconut, pineapple juice, and Puerto Rican rums turns out to be the most refreshing natural tropical cocktail you'll ever have. As a matter of fact, only the original Coco Lopez cream of coconut meets the necessary conditions of flavor and consistency to prepare the perfect piña colada.

Coco Lopez Piña Colada Goes International

Tourists that came to Puerto Rico and tasted a piña colada became true fans, and they took Coco Lopez back home so they could again enjoy "The Taste of the Tropics."

Today, Coco Lopez has expanded the distribution into over fifty countries around the world. You can find it in Europe, the Middle East, Japan, Central and South America, the United States, and as close as your nearest supermarket.

Enjoy an Original

Original Piña Colada

4 oz. Coco Lopez cream of coconut
4 oz. pineapple juice
2 oz. Puerto Rican rum
2 cups crushed ice

Mix well in blender. Garnish with a cherry and pineapple. Serves two.

Family Piña Colada
For a refreshing piña colada the whole family will enjoy, just leave out the rum.

Blender Drinks from A to Z
All cocktails should be blended with ice

A Day at the Beach

1 oz. Disaronno amaretto
1 oz. orange juice
splash grenadine
1/2 oz. pineapple juice

Abbot's Delight

2 oz. Frangelico
1/2 oz. small ripe banana, sliced
1/4 cup pineapple juice
1/3 cup ice, crushed
2 dashes Angostura bitters

Aberdeen Sour

1 1/2 oz. Cutty Sark
1/2 oz. Hiram Walker triple sec
1 oz. orange juice
1 oz. lemon juice

Absolut Citron Colada

1 1/2 oz. Absolut Citron
1 oz. crème de banana
2 oz. pineapple juice
2 oz. Coco Lopez cream of coconut
2 tbs. lime juice
2 tbs. sugar

Garnish with pineapple and coconut slices.

Absolut Kurant Freeze

1 1/2 oz. Absolut Kurant
1/2 oz. crème de banana
3 fresh raspberries
1 fresh banana
2 tbs. sugar

Absolut Stress

1 oz. Absolut vodka
1/2 oz. peach schnapps
1 oz. cranberry juice
1 oz. pineapple juice
1/2 oz. Coco Lopez cream of coconut

Garnish with a maraschino cherry.

Absolutely Awesome Orange

3 oz. Bartenders Awesome orange cream
1 oz. Absolut Mandrin

Tim Lowery, WI

Acapulco Gold

1 1/4 oz. Jose Cuervo Especial tequila
5/8 oz. Grand Marnier
1 oz. sweet & sour mix

Agent Orange

1 oz. vodka
1 oz. Yukon Jack
1/2 oz. apple schnapps
1/2 oz. melon liqueur
1/4 oz. grenadine
2 oz. orange juice

Aggravation

1 oz. Kahlúa
1/2 oz. scotch
2 oz. cream

Alaskan Blue Whale

1 1/2 oz. gin
1 oz. blue curacao
1 oz. Coco Lopez cream of coconut

©2000 Vita-Mix Corporation

Albatross Sea Breeze

1 1/2 oz. Midori melon liqueur
1 oz. gin
2 oz. fresh lime juice
1 egg white

Albino Eskimo

1 oz. Kahlúa
1/2 oz. strawberry schnapps
1/2 oz. amaretto
1 1/2 oz. cream or milk

Garnish with a strawberry.

Alexander's Sister

2 oz. gin
1 oz. white crème de menthe
3 oz. whipping cream or heavy cream

Ali-Colada

2 oz. Alizé
dash Bacardi rum
2 oz. Coco Lopez cream of coconut

Garnish with a pineapple wedge.

Alien Urine Sample

1/4 oz. Midori melon liqueur
3/4 oz. peach schnapps
3/4 oz. Malibu rum
3/4 oz. crème de banana
1 oz. sweet & sour mix
blue curacao

Float blue curacao.

Alizé Dreamsicle

1 1/2 oz. Alizé
1/2 oz. Absolut vodka
2 oz. pineapple juice
2 oz. orange juice
1/2 oz. Coco Lopez cream of coconut
1 tbs. Major Peters' grenadine

Almond Joy

1 oz. Hiram Walker amaretto
1 oz. Hiram Walker white crème de cacao
2 oz. cream

Aloha

1 oz. dark rum
1/2 oz. lime juice
2 oz. pineapple juice
2 oz. fresh orange juice
1 oz. Coco Lopez cream of coconut
1 small scoop vanilla ice cream

Garnish with a pineapple spear and maraschino cherry.

Ambrosia Punch

20 oz. can crushed pineapple, undrained
15 oz. Coco Lopez cream of coconut
2 cups apricot nectar, chilled
2 cups orange juice, chilled
1 1/2 cups light rum
1 liter club soda, chilled

In a blender, puree the pineapple and cream of coconut until smooth. In a punch bowl, combine the pureed mixture, nectar, juice, and rum. Mix well.

Just before serving, add club soda and serve over ice. Serves 15–20.

An Alternate Root

1 1/2 oz. Hiram Walker Old Fashioned
   root beer schnapps
3 oz. orange juice

Angostura Sundae

1 oz. gold rum
2 scoops vanilla ice cream
1/2 tsp. Angostura bitters

Garnish with a maraschino cherry.

Aphrodite's Lover Potion

1 1/2 oz. Metaxa brandy
3 oz. pineapple juice

Apple Daiquiri

1 oz. apple schnapps
1 oz. light rum
1/2 oz. sweet & sour mix
1/4 peeled apple

Apple Graham Crispy

1 oz. apple schnapps
1/2 oz. brandy
1/2 oz. Irish cream
2 scoops vanilla ice cream
1/4 cup graham cracker crumbs

Blend first four ingredients. Sprinkle with graham cracker crumbs.

Apple Hummer

1 1/2 oz. DeKuyper apple barrel
   schnapps
1 oz. Gilbey's rum
1 scoop vanilla ice cream

Garnish with a maraschino cherry.

Appleton V/X Orange Daiquiri

1 oz. Appleton Estate V/X Jamaican rum
juice of 1 orange
juice of 1/4 lime
1 tsp. sugar

Garnish with a sprig of mint and an orange rind.

Appleton V/X Piña Colada

2 oz. Appleton Estate V/X Jamaican rum
2 oz. pineapple juice
3/4 oz. sweet cream
3/4 oz. coconut cream

Garnish with a pineapple spear and maraschino cherry.

Apricot Colada

1 1/2 oz. Hiram Walker apricot brandy
3 oz. Coco Lopez cream of coconut
2 oz. vanilla ice cream

Apricot Piña

1 1/2 oz. light rum
1/2 oz. apricot brandy
1 1/2 oz. unsweetened pineapple juice
1 oz. Coco Lopez cream of coconut

Apricot Sunset

2 oz. Marie Brizard apricot liqueur
1 oz. orange juice
1 oz. lemon juice
1 oz. cranberry juice
few drops gin

April Shower

1 1/2 oz. Bacardi Silver rum
3 oz. pink grapefruit juice, chilled

Ariana's Dream

1 oz. Alizé
1 oz. crème de cacao
1/2 oz. Bacardi
3 oz. orange juice

Garnish with a fresh strawberry.

Bacardi Alexander

3/4 oz. Bacardi rum
1/2 oz. dark crème de cacao
1/2 oz. cream or 2 scoops ice cream
nutmeg garnish

Bacardi Amber Daiquiri

2 oz. Bacardi dark rum
2 tsp. fresh lime or lemon juice
1/2 tsp. sugar
1/2 tsp. cream
nutmeg garnish

Bacardi Banana Colada

1 1/2 oz. Bacardi light or dark rum
1/2 ripe banana
1 oz. Coco Lopez cream of coconut
banana wedge (optional)

Serve with a wedge of banana, if desired.

Bacardi Banana Daiquiri

1 1/2 tsp. Bacardi light
1/3 ripe banana
1 tsp. sugar
1/2 tsp. lime or lemon juice

Bacardi Beachcomber

1 1/2 oz. Bacardi light or dark rum
1 oz. lemon or lime juice
1/2 oz. cherry liqueur

Bacardi Big Apple

1 1/2 oz. Bacardi light or dark rum
3/4 oz. lemon or lime juice
1/2 oz. apple brandy
3/4 oz. grenadine
apple wedge (optional)

Garnish with a slice of apple.

Bacardi Black Dirty Colada

1 1/4 oz. Bacardi black rum
1 oz. Coco Lopez cream of coconut
2 oz. pineapple juice

Bacardi Blossom

1 1/4 oz. Bacardi light rum
1 oz. orange juice
1/2 oz. lemon juice
1/2 tsp. sugar

Bacardi Cocktail

1 1/2 oz. Bacardi light rum
1 oz. lime juice
1/2 tsp. sugar
1/2 oz. grenadine

Bacardi Daiquiri*

1 1/2 oz. Bacardi light rum
1/2 oz. lime or lemon juice
1/2 tsp. sugar

*The original daiquiri was made with Bacardi
rum in 1896.*

Bacardi Grasshopper

1 oz. Bacardi light rum
1/4 oz. green crème de menthe
1/2 oz. cream

Bacardi Hemingway

1 1/2 oz. Bacardi light rum
juice of 1/2 lime
1/4 oz. grapefruit juice
1/4 oz. maraschino liqueur

Bacardi Key Largo

1 1/2 oz. Bacardi black rum
2 oz. orange juice
1 1/2 oz. coconut cream

Garnish with a maraschino cherry.

Bacardi Orange Bowl

1 1/2 oz. Bacardi light rum
1 oz. orange juice
1 oz. cream, milk, or half-and-half

Garnish with an orange section, if desired.

Bacardi Orange Daiquiri

1 1/2 oz. Bacardi light rum
2 tsp. lime or lemon juice
1 oz. orange juice
1 tsp. sugar

Bacardi Peach Daiquiri

2 oz. Bacardi light rum
2 tsp. fresh, peeled peach halves
1 tsp. sugar
1 oz. lime or lemon juice

Bacardi Piña Colada

1 1/4 oz. Bacardi light-dry or gold rum
2 oz. unsweetened pineapple juice
1 oz. Coco Lopez cream of coconut

Bacardi Pineapple Daiquiri

2 oz. Bacardi light rum
1/2 slice canned pineapple
1 tbs. lime juice
1 tsp. sugar

Bacardi Rum Runner

1 1/4 oz. Bacardi dark rum
1/2 oz. blackberry brandy
1/2 oz. banana liqueur
1/8 oz. grenadine
1/2 oz. lime juice

Bacardi Stinger

2 oz. Bacardi dark rum
1 oz. white crème de menthe

Bacardi Strawberry Daiquiri

1 1/2 tsp. Bacardi light rum
5 oz. fresh or frozen whole strawberries
1 tbs. lime juice
1 tsp. sugar

Garnish with a whole strawberry.

Bahama Mama

1/2 oz. light rum
2 oz. apple juice
1/2 oz. Coco Lopez cream of coconut
1 oz. orange juice
dash Angostura grenadine
dash triple sec

Baileys Alexander

1/2 oz. Baileys Irish cream
1/2 oz. white crème de cacao
1/2 oz. cognac

Baileys Banana Blaster

1 oz. Baileys Irish cream
1 oz. Malibu rum
1/2 oz. banana liqueur or 1/2 banana

Baileys Blizzard

1 oz. Baileys Irish cream
1/2 oz. peppermint schnapps
1/2 oz. brandy
3 oz. vanilla ice cream

Garnish with a maraschino cherry.

Baileys Blizzard II

1 oz. Baileys Irish cream
1/2 oz. Rumple Minze
1/2 oz. Metaxa brandy

Baileys Chill-Out Cappuccino

4 parts double-strength coffee
1 1/2 oz. Baileys Irish cream
1 part cream
2 tsp. sugar

Top with whipped cream and sprinkle with cinnamon or cocoa powder.

Baileys Coconut Frappe

2 oz. Baileys Irish cream
1 oz. Malibu rum
2 oz. milk

Garnish with toasted coconut.

Baileys Cream Dream

2 oz. Baileys Irish cream
2 oz. half-and-half

Baileys Dream Shake

2 oz. Baileys Irish cream
2 scoops vanilla ice cream

Garnish with a maraschino cherry.

Baileys Float

2 oz. Baileys Irish cream
2 scoops softened ice cream

Blend and top with one more scoop of ice cream.

Baileys French Dream

1 1/2 oz. Baileys Irish cream
1/2 oz. raspberry liqueur
2 oz. half-and-half

Baileys Frozen Mudslide

1 oz. Baileys Irish cream
1 oz. coffee liqueur
1 oz. Stolichnaya vodka

Baileys Iced Cappuccino

Brew a pot of double-strength coffee and set aside to cool. In a blender combine:

1/2 cup ice
2 oz. Baileys Irish cream
3 oz. double-strength coffee
1 oz. half-and-half
2 tsp. sugar

Baileys Italian Dream

1 1/2 oz. Baileys Irish cream
1/2 oz. Disaronno amaretto
2 oz. half-and-half

Baileys Light Shake

2 oz. Baileys Irish cream light
2 large scoops vanilla frozen yogurt

Baileys Malibu Slide

1 oz. Baileys Irish cream
1 oz. Kahlúa
1 oz. Malibu rum

Baileys Rum Yum

1 oz. Baileys Irish cream
1 oz. Malibu rum
1 oz. cream or milk

Garnish with a maraschino cherry.

Baileys Russian Dream

1 1/2 oz. Baileys Irish cream
1/2 oz. vodka
2 oz. half-and-half

Bali Dream

1 oz. white rum
1/2 oz. dark rum
1/2 oz. crème de banana
1 oz. Coco Lopez cream of coconut
splash grenadine
1 oz. orange juice

Ballsbridge Bracer

3/4 oz. Irish Mist
1 oz. Tullamore Dew Irish whiskey
3 oz. orange juice
1 egg white

Banana B. Jones

1 1/2 oz. crème de banana
1 oz. Coco Lopez cream of coconut
1 scoop vanilla ice cream
1 banana

Top with whipped cream. Garnish with a banana slice and maraschino cherry.

Banana Banshee

1 1/2 oz. crème de banana
1/2 oz. white crème de cacao
1 scoop vanilla ice cream

Banana Boat

1 1/2 oz. tequila
1/2 oz. banana liqueur
1 oz. lime juice

Banana Chi Chi

2 oz. Coco Lopez cream of coconut
1 1/2 oz. pineapple juice
1 1/2 oz. vodka
1/2 banana

Mix until smooth.

Banana Colada

2 oz. Coco Lopez cream of coconut
1 1/2 oz. rum
1 medium banana
1 tsp. lemon juice

Mix until smooth.

Banana Cow

1 1/2 oz. Puerto Rican rum
1 tsp. banana, ripe
2 tsp. bar sugar
3 oz. milk

Banana Cream Pie

1 oz. vodka
1/2 oz. Irish cream
1/2 oz. banana liqueur
1/2 ripe banana, peeled
1 scoop vanilla ice cream

Banana Daiquiri

1 1/2 oz. light rum
1/2 oz. lime juice
1 oz. banana liqueur
1/4 banana, sliced
1 tsp. sugar or honey (optional)
1/2 oz. cream

Banana Daiquiribe

2 oz. CocoRibe
1 very ripe banana
1/2 oz. lime juice

Banana Di Amore

1 oz. amaretto
1/2 oz. crème de banana
2 oz. orange juice
1 oz. sweet & sour mix

Banana Frosted

1 oz. Disaronno amaretto
1/2 ripe banana
2 scoops vanilla or banana ice cream
1/2 cup milk

Banana Lemon Cooler

1 1/2 oz. Bacardi light rum
1/4 ripe banana
3/4 oz. lemon juice
3/4 oz. pineapple juice

Top with lemon soda.

Banana Lopez

2 oz. Coco Lopez cream of coconut
1 medium banana
1 tsp. lemon juice

Banana Mama

1 1/2 oz. light rum
1/2 oz. dark rum
1 oz. banana liqueur
1 oz. Coco Lopez cream of coconut
1 oz. fresh or frozen strawberries
2 oz. pineapple juice

Banana Margarita

2 oz. DeKuyper crème de banana
1 oz. Sauza tequila
1/2 oz. DeKuyper triple sec
1 oz. freshly squeezed lime juice

Banana Punch Frappe

1 1/2 oz. Bacardi light rum
3/4 oz. orange juice
1/2 oz. banana liqueur

Banana Rama

1 oz. Kahlúa
1/2 oz. crème de banana
1/2 oz. crème de almond
2 oz. half-and-half

Banana Split

1/4 oz. Kahlúa
1/4 oz. crème de banana
1/4 oz. crème de almond
half-and-half

*Garnish with whipped cream, a maraschino cherry,
and/or a banana slice.*

Banana Tree

1 oz. banana liqueur
1/2 oz. crème de banana
1/4 oz. crème de almond
half-and-half

Garnish with whipped cream, maraschino cherry, and/or a banana slice.

Banilla Boat

1 oz. Drambuie
1/2 oz. Hiram Walker crème de banana
4 oz. vanilla ice cream

Banshee

1 oz. banana liqueur
1/2 oz. white crème de cacao
1 scoop vanilla ice cream
1 whole ripe banana, peeled

Garnish with banana.

Barbados Cocktail

2 oz. Mount Gay rum
1/2 oz. Cointreau
1/2 oz. sweet & sour mix

Barbary Coast

1/2 oz. Cutty Sark
1/2 oz. Beefeater dry gin
1/2 oz. Hiram Walker white crème de cacao
1/2 oz. heavy cream

Bareback Rider

2 oz. Mandarine Napoleon
1 tsp. sugar
juice of 1/2 lime

Top with two maraschino cherries.

Barefoot Boy with Bongo

1 1/2 oz. Campari
1 oz. rye
1/2 oz. dry vermouth

Garnish with a twist of lemon peel.

Basic Daiquiri

2 oz. white rum
1 oz. lime juice
1 tbs. sugar

Batida Abaci

2 oz. cachaca or light rum
1/2 cup pineapple chunks

Bay Bomber

1/4 oz. vodka
1/4 oz. gin
1/4 oz. rum
1/4 oz. tequila
1/4 oz. triple sec
1 oz. orange juice
1 oz. pineapple juice
1 oz. cranberry juice
1 oz. sweet & sour mix

Blend and float a splash of 151-proof rum on top.

Bayou Juice

1 oz. rum
1 oz. amaretto
1 oz. cranberry juice
1 oz. pineapple juice
1 oz. Coco Lopez cream of coconut

Beach Bum's Cooler

1 1/4 oz. Irish cream
3/4 oz. light rum
1/4 oz. banana liqueur
1 1/2 oz. Coco Lopez cream of coconut
1/4 banana
2 scoops vanilla ice cream

Garnish with a maraschino cherry.

Beach Party

1 1/2 oz. Bacardi light or dark rum
1 oz. pineapple juice
1 oz. lemon or lime juice
1 oz. orange juice
1 oz. grenadine

Beachcomber

1 oz. Galliano
1 oz. triple sec
4 oz. orange juice
1 oz. half-and-half

Beachcomber's Golddust

1 1/2 oz. light rum
1 oz. lime juice
1/2 oz. triple sec
1 oz. Coco Lopez cream of coconut
1/2 tsp. sugar

Beachcomber's Special

1 1/2 oz. Bacardi light rum
1/2 oz. orange curacao
3/4 oz. lemon or lime juice
1/4 tsp. sugar (optional)

Beachside Coco Lopez

1 1/2 oz. Midori melon liqueur
1 oz. Bacardi light rum
3 oz. Coco Lopez cream of coconut
2 oz. Coco Lopez strawberry daiquiri mix

Bean Stalk

1 1/4 oz. Kahlúa
3/4 oz. rum
4 oz. cream

Beaujolais Cocktail

4 oz. Beaujolais
1/4 oz. red seedless grapes
1/2 scoop rainbow sherbet
1/4 cup ice cubes

Blend until smooth. Garnish with red seedless grapes.

©2000 Vita-Mix Corporation

Bee Bite Cocktail

1 oz. light rum
juice of 2 limes
2 oz. orange juice
2 tsp. grenadine

Beefeater Blue Devil

1 oz. Beefeater dry gin
1/4 oz. lemon juice
dash maraschino liqueur
dash Hiram Walker blue curacao
dash powdered sugar

Bellini 2000

1 oz. Cruzan pineapple rum
2 oz. sparkling wine
2 oz. peach schnapps
spoonful Coco Lopez cream of coconut

Float Alizé.

Bermuda Triangle

1 1/2 oz. Gosling's Black Seal rum
2 oz. cranberry juice
2 oz. orange juice

Berry-Cherry Cream

1 1/2 oz. crème de cassis
1 1/2 oz. chocolate cherry liqueur
3 oz. vanilla ice cream

Garnish with a maraschino cherry.

Big Apple

2 oz. apple brandy
1/2 oz. amaretto
3 oz. apple juice
1 tbs. applesauce

Garnish with ground cinnamon.

Big Blue Sky

1/2 oz. light rum
1/2 oz. blue curacao
1/2 oz. Coco Lopez cream of coconut
2 oz. pineapple juice

Bikini Daiquiri

3/4 oz. Cruzan pineapple rum
3/4 oz. Cruzan banana rum
2 oz. Coco Lopez cream of coconut
1 oz. lime juice

Bikini

1 shot vodka
1/2 shot peach schnapps
2 oz. peach nectar
2 oz. orange juice
splash lemon juice
1 oz. champagne, chilled

Blend the first five ingredients, then add champagne.

Bishop Cocktail

1 1/2 oz. Bacardi light or dark rum
3/4 oz. red wine
3/4 oz. lemon or lime juice
1 tsp. sugar (optional)

Bit O' Honey

1 oz. Baileys Irish cream
1 oz. white crème de menthe
2 scoops vanilla ice cream

Garnish with a maraschino cherry.

Black Forest

1 oz. vodka
1/2 oz. coffee liqueur
1/2 oz. Chambord
1 scoop chocolate ice cream

Garnish with shaved chocolate or sprinkles.

Black Rose

1/2 oz. gold tequila
1/2 oz. Kahlúa
1/2 oz. Chambord
1/2 cup fresh or frozen strawberries
1 1/2 oz. cream or milk

Black Rum Runner

2 oz. Bacardi black rum
3 oz. Coco Lopez rum runner mix

Black Seal Rum Runner

1 1/4 oz. Gosling's Black Seal rum
3/4 oz. blackberry liqueur
1 oz. banana liqueur
3/4 oz. grenadine
1/2 oz. lime juice

Blackberry Cream

1 1/2 oz. Hiram Walker blackberry
  brandy
4 oz. cream

Blackthorn

1 1/2 oz. Irish whiskey
1 1/2 oz. dry vermouth
3–4 dashes Pernod
3–4 dashes Angostura bitters

Sloe gin can be used in place of Irish whiskey.

Blizzard

1 1/2 oz. bourbon
1 1/2 oz. cranberry juice
1/2 oz. lime juice
1/2 oz. grenadine
1 tsp. sugar

Bloodhound

2 oz. gin
1 oz. dry vermouth
1 oz. sweet vermouth
3 fresh strawberry halves

Blue Bayou

1 oz. Malibu rum
1/2 oz. DeKuyper blueberry schnapps
1/2 oz. blue curacao
3 oz. sweet & sour mix

Blue Gillati

1/2 oz. vodka
1/2 oz. DeKuyper blueberry schnapps
1/2 oz. Midori melon liqueur
1/2 oz. blue curacao
sweet & sour mix

Blue Hawaiian

1 1/2 oz. light rum
1 oz. blue curacao
2 oz. Coco Lopez cream of coconut
3 oz. pineapple juice

Blue Hawaiian II

1 1/2 oz. Malibu rum
1/2 oz. blue curacao
4 oz. pineapple juice
splash sweet & sour mix

Blue Heaven

1 oz. Hiram Walker blue curacao
1 oz. light rum
1 oz. pineapple juice
1 tsp. Coco Lopez cream of coconut

Blue Margarita

1 1/2 oz. tequila
1/2 oz. blue curacao
1 tsp. triple sec
1 oz. lime juice or juice of 1/2 lime

Rim the glass with salt and a lime wedge.

Blue Moon Margaritas

2 oz. 100% silver agave tequila
1 oz. blue curacao
1/4 oz. Grand Marnier
2 oz. sweet & sour mix
1/8 oz. Rose's sweetened lime juice
lime wedge

Blue Sky

1 1/2 oz. Canadian Mist
3/4 oz. Bacardi light rum
3/4 oz. blue curacao
8 oz. pineapple juice

Garnish with an orange slice and a maraschino cherry.

Blue Tail Butterfly

1 oz. blue curacao
1 oz. white crème de cacao
3 oz. vanilla ice cream

Blue Whale

1 oz. gin
3/4 oz. curacao
1 oz. Coco Lopez cream of coconut

Blueberries and Cream

1 1/2 oz. blueberry schnapps
2 oz. Coco Lopez cream of coconut
1/2 oz. cream

Blueberry & Cream

1 1/2 oz. DeKuyper blueberry schnapps
1 oz. cream or half-and-half

Blueberry Daiquiri

2 oz. Bacardi light rum
1 oz. blueberry schnapps
1 oz. lemon or lime juice
1/2 cup blueberries

Blushin' Russian

1 oz. Kahlúa
3/4 oz. vodka
3 oz. vanilla ice cream
splash of grenadine

Blushing Bride Cocktail

2 oz. Romana sambuca
1 oz. sloe gin

Boarsenberry

1 1/2 oz. Gordon's wildberry vodka
3/4 oz. Chambord
1/2 oz. Frangelico
1/4 oz. crème de noyaux
half-and-half, cream, or vanilla ice cream

Float blackberries and sprinkle with nutmeg.

Bobby Buttercream

3 oz. Southern Comfort
6 scoops butter pecan ice cream
1/4 tsp. maple flavoring

Bossa Nova

2 oz. dark rum
1 1/2 oz. Galliano
1 oz. apricot brandy
3 oz. passion fruit juice

Boston Breeze

1 1/4 oz. rum
1 oz. Coco Lopez cream of coconut
3 oz. cranberry juice cocktail

Boston Flip

1 oz. madeira wine
1 oz. bourbon
1 egg yolk
1/2 tsp. maple flavoring

Boston Southside

1 1/2 oz. gin
1 1/2 oz. sweet & sour mix
1/2 oz. lime juice
1/2 tsp. sugar

Bourbon Slush

1 1/2 oz. bourbon
2 oz. sweetened tea
1/2 oz. orange juice
1 oz. lemonade

Bow Street Special

1 1/2 oz. Tullamore Dew
1/2 oz. Hiram Walker triple sec
1 oz. lemon juice

Brandied Peaches & Cream

1 oz. peach schnapps
3/4 oz. brandy
1 1/2 oz. Coco Lopez cream of coconut
1 scoop vanilla ice cream

Garnish with a maraschino cherry.

Brandy and Rum

2 oz. brandy
1 1/2 oz. light rum
1 tbs. lemon juice
1 egg yolk
1 tsp. bar sugar

Brandy Bracer

2 oz. brandy
2 dashes anisette
2 dashes Angostura bitters
1 tsp. lemon juice
1 tsp. sugar
1 egg

Brandy Cobbler

1/2 tsp. sugar
2 oz. brandy
1 tsp. blue curacao or triple sec

Brandy Collins

2 oz. brandy
1 tsp. sugar
1/2 lemon, peeled

Brandy Daisy

2 oz. brandy
1 tsp. grenadine
juice of 1/2 lemon

Blend and top with club soda.

Brandy Egg Nog

1 oz. brandy
1 oz. Jamaican rum
1 whole egg
2 oz. milk
1 tsp. bar sugar

Brandy Ice

1 1/2 oz. brandy
1/2 oz. white crème de cacao
2 oz. vanilla ice cream

Garnish with a maraschino cherry.

Brown Bomber

1 oz. DeKuyper root beer schnapps
1 oz. DeKuyper crème de cacao
2 oz. half-and-half or heavy cream

Brown Cow

1 1/2 oz. root beer schnapps
3 oz. vanilla ice cream

Blend and top with root beer.

Brown Derby

1 1/2 oz. Bacardi dark rum
3/4 oz. lemon or lime juice
1 tsp. maple syrup

Brunswick Sour

1 1/2 oz. Bacardi light rum
3/4 oz. lime juice
1/2 tsp. sugar

Blend and float Claret wine.

Bugsy's Baccio

3/4 oz. Disaronno amaretto
3 mini Lazzaroni Amaretti cookies
1/2 oz. Malibu rum
1/2 oz. crème de cacao
1 oz. cranberry juice
2 scoops vanilla ice cream

Bull Fighter

1 1/2 oz. Sauza Hornitos tequila
2 oz. pineapple juice
1 oz. Rose's lime juice
1/2 oz. grenadine

Bulldog Cocktail

1 1/2 oz. Bacardi light or dark rum
3/4 oz. lime juice
1/2 oz. cherry brandy

Garnish with a maraschino cherry.

Bumble Bee Stinger

3/4 oz. Galliano
1 oz. Rémy Martin cognac
1/2 oz. Pernod

Bunny Bonanza

2 oz. gold tequila
1 oz. apple brandy
1/2 oz. lemon juice
3/4 tsp. maple syrup
3 dashes triple sec

Garnish with a lemon slice.

Burnt Almond

1 oz. vodka
1 oz. Kahlúa
1/2 oz. amaretto
1 scoop vanilla ice cream

Bushwacker

2 oz. Kahlúa
1/2 oz. Hiram Walker dark crème de cacao
1/2 oz. Bacardi black rum
2 oz. Coco Lopez cream of coconut
2 oz. half-and-half

Busted Cherry

1 oz. light rum
1/2 oz. dark crème de cacao
1/2 oz. amaretto
2 oz. cherry juice
3 maraschino cherries
cream

Garnish with whipped cream and a maraschino cherry in a hurricane glass.

Jerry Wood
Phoenix, AZ

Butterfly Milk Punch

2 oz. cognac
dash Angostura bitters
1 oz. crème de cacao
3 oz. milk
1/2 tsp. bar sugar

Cacao Mint

1 oz. Hiram Walker spearmint schnapps
1 oz. Hiram Walker white crème de cacao
3 oz. vanilla ice cream

Garnish with a maraschino cherry.

Cactus Colada

1 1/4 oz. tequila
3/4 oz. Midori melon liqueur
2 oz. Coco Lopez cream of coconut
1 oz. orange juice
1 oz. pineapple juice
1/2 oz. grenadine

California Coastline

1 oz. Malibu rum
1 oz. peach schnapps
1/2 oz. blue curacao
2 oz. pineapple juice

Garnish with a pineapple slice.

California Fizz

1 1/2 oz. Bacardi light or dark rum
1 egg
4 oz. orange juice

Calm Voyage

1 oz. Bacardi light-dry or gold rum
1/4 oz. Hiram Walker apple brandy
1 oz. orange juice
dash bitters

Calypso Cool-Aid

1 1/4 oz. Rhum Barbancourt
1 oz. pineapple juice
1/2 oz. lemon or lime juice
1/4 tsp. sugar

*Blend and top with club soda. Garnish with a
pineapple spear and a lime wheel.*

Calypso Daiquiri

1 1/2 oz. Myers's Jamaican rum
1 ripe banana
1 tsp. vanilla extract
1 1/2 oz. sweet & sour mix
1/2 oz. half-and-half

Garnish with tropical fruit.

Calypso Highway

1 oz. light rum
1/2 oz. blue curacao
1/2 oz. crème de banana
2 oz. Coco Lopez cream of coconut
2 oz. orange juice
2 oz. pineapple juice

Camino Real

1 1/2 oz. Gran Centenario Plata or
 reposado tequila
1/2 oz. banana liqueur
1 oz. orange juice
dash lime juice
dash coconut milk

Garnish with a lime slice.

Candy

1 oz. Galliano
1 oz. Rémy Martin cognac
dash maraschino liqueur
2 scoops orange sherbet

Garnish with chocolate chips or chocolate curls.

Canyon Quake

3/4 oz. Irish cream
3/4 oz. brandy
1/2 oz. amaretto
2 oz. light cream

Garnish with a maraschino cherry.

Cape Colada

1 oz. vodka
1/2 oz. peach schnapps
1 oz. Coco Lopez cream of coconut
1 oz. cranberry juice
1 oz. sweet & sour mix

Captain Caribbean

3 oz. Kahlúa
1 1/2 oz. coconut rum
splash Galliano

Garnish with pineapple, orange, and banana slices.

Captain Morgan Planter's Punch

1 1/4 oz. Captain Morgan spiced rum
3 oz. orange juice
1/2 oz. lemon or lime juice
1 tsp. sugar
dash grenadine

Captain Morgan Spiced Rum Daiquiri

1 1/4 oz. Captain Morgan spiced rum
juice of 1/2 lime
1 tsp. sugar

Captain Morgan Spiced Rum Piña Colada

1 1/4 oz. Captain Morgan spiced rum
1 oz. Coco Lopez cream of coconut
2 oz. pineapple juice, unsweetened

Captain Morgan's Fruit Daiquiri

1 1/4 oz. Captain Morgan spiced rum
juice of 1/2 lime
1 tsp. sugar

Add basic daiquiri ingredients plus either five large strawberries, 1/2 ripe banana, 1/2 peach (peeled), or 1/2 sliced canned pineapple.

Captain Morgan's Spyglass

1 oz. Captain Morgan spiced rum
2 scoops vanilla ice cream
1 tbs. honey
dash milk (optional)

Captain's Cream Delight

1 1/4 oz. Captain Morgan spiced rum
1 oz. Coco Lopez cream of coconut
2 oz. orange juice

Captain's Parrot

1 shot Captain Morgan spiced rum
1 shot Parrot Bay
6 oz. pineapple juice
2 oz. orange juice

Blend with ice. Float 1 tablespoon maraschino cherry juice on top. Garnish with maraschino cherries.

Robert R. Towson
Newark, DE

Captain's Berry Daiquiri

1 1/4 oz. Captain Morgan spiced rum
1/2 cup strawberries or raspberries
1 tsp. lime juice
1/2 tsp. sugar

Garnish with berries.

Captain's Colada

1 1/4 oz. Captain Morgan spiced rum
1 oz. Coco Lopez cream of coconut
3 oz. pineapple juice (unsweetened)

Garnish with a pineapple spear and maraschino cherry.

Captain's Daiquiri

1 1/4 oz. Captain Morgan spiced rum
2 tsp. lime juice
1/2 tsp. sugar

Garnish with a lime wedge.

Captain's Morgarita

1 oz. Captain Morgan spiced rum
1/2 oz. triple sec
3 oz. frozen limeade

Carabinieri

3/4 oz. Galliano
1 oz. tequila
1/4 oz. lemon juice
2 3/4 oz. orange juice
1 egg yolk

Cardinal's Cocktail

1 1/2 oz. Bacardi light rum
1 oz. lime juice
1/4 oz. triple sec
1/4 oz. grenadine
1/4 oz. orgeat syrup

Caribbean Colada

1 1/2 oz. Rhum Grandier
4 oz. pineapple juice
1 1/2 oz. Coco Lopez cream of coconut

Garnish with a pineapple spear.

Caribbean Cruise

1 oz. dark rum
1 oz. coffee liqueur
2 oz. Coco Lopez cream of coconut
3 oz. pineapple juice
1 oz. half-and-half

Caribbean Frost

1 1/2 oz. vodka (flavored vodka can be used)
4 oz. Coco Lopez cream of coconut

Caribbean Grasshopper

1 oz. white crème de cacao
1/2 oz. green crème de menthe
1 1/2 oz. Coco Lopez cream of coconut

Caribbean Gridlock

1/2 oz. Bacardi light rum
1/2 oz. Mount Gay Eclipse rum
1/2 oz. Cruzan Estate Diamond rum
1/2 oz. Grand Marnier
2 oz. sweet & sour mix
1/2 cup raspberries

Serve a shot of Chambord on the side.

Caribbean Joy

1 1/2 oz. Bacardi light rum
1 oz. pineapple juice
3/4 oz. lemon juice

Caribbean Passion

3/4 oz. Passoã
1/2 oz. Mount Gay rum
1 oz. pineapple juice
splash orange juice

Caribbean Queen

1 1/4 oz. Bacardi Limon
1/2 oz. Cointreau
2 oz. orange juice
3 oz. Coco Lopez cream of coconut

Caribbean Queen II

1 1/2 oz. watermelon schnapps
1 oz. Coco Lopez cream of coconut
1/4 oz. triple sec
2 oz. orange juice
2 oz. lemonade

Caribbean Romance

3 oz. Bacardi Superior white rum
1 1/2 oz. sugar syrup
2 pieces papaya
2 pieces banana
1 oz. lime juice
1 oz. Coco Lopez cream of coconut

Garnish with orange, pineapple, and a cherry.

Caribbean Sunset

2 1/2 oz. Bacardi
1 1/2 oz. Coco Lopez cream of coconut
1 1/2 oz. carrot juice
2 1/2 oz. strawberry concentrate
1 1/2 oz. coconut water
1 1/2 oz. mango puree

Garnish with mango and cherry/palm tree stir stick.

Caribbean Welcome

1 1/2 oz. Bacardi light rum
1 oz. apricot brandy
1 oz. Coco Lopez cream of coconut
1 oz. pineapple juice

Garnish with a maraschino cherry.

Carousel

2 oz. Mandarine Napoleon
2 oz. gin
1 oz. lemon juice

Cassie's Delight

2 oz. Baileys Irish cream
1 1/2 oz. Kahlúa
1/2 oz. crème de cacao
1 oz. milk

Catalina Margarita

1 1/4 oz. Jose Cuervo gold tequila
1 oz. peach schnapps
1 oz. blue curacao
4 oz. sweet & sour mix

Catherine Was Great!

1 oz. Stoli Strasberi vodka
1/2 oz. Disaronno amaretto
1/2 oz. light rum
1 tsp. triple sec
2 oz. orange juice

Cavalier

1 1/2 oz. Sauza tequila
1/2 oz. Galliano
1 1/2 oz. orange juice
1/2 oz. cream

Garnish with a maraschino cherry.

CC Cider

1 oz. Canadian Club
1/2 oz. Hiram Walker cinnamon schnapps
3 oz. apple cider
1/4 unpeeled red apple

Celtic Crush

Equal parts:
  Celtic Crossing
  orange juice

Chambord Colada

1 1/2 oz. Chambord
1 1/2 oz. Bacardi rum
2 oz. pineapple juice
1/2 oz. Coco Lopez cream of coconut

Chambord Frost

1 1/2 oz. Chambord
juice of 1/2 lemon

Chambord Margarita

1 oz. gold tequila
1/2 oz. triple sec
1/2 oz. Chambord
3 oz. margarita mix

Chamborlada

1 oz. Chambord
1/2 oz. Bacardi light rum
1/2 oz. Bacardi dark rum
3 oz. pineapple juice
2 oz. Coco Lopez cream of coconut

Cherry Alexander

3/4 oz. premium brandy
3/4 oz. crème de cacao
1/2 oz. cherry brandy or cherry juice
6 maraschino cherries
splash half-and-half

Serve in a brandy snifter. Garnish with shaved chocolate or chocolate curls and a maraschino cherry.

Heidi Epling
Seattle, WA

Cherry Amaretto Freeze

2 oz. amaretto
4 scoops ice cream
10 maraschino cherries

Blend and serve.

Michael Manganaro
Metairie, LA

Cherry Amore

1 oz. cherry heering
1/2 oz. amaretto
1/2 oz. vodka
2 scoops vanilla ice cream
4 maraschino cherries

Top with whipped cream and maraschino cherries.

Les Hemingway
Cincinnati, OH

Cherry Blossom

2 jiggers sloe gin
1 oz. orange juice
1 tbs. lemon juice
1 tbs. maraschino cherry juice or cherry liqueur

Garnish with a maraschino cherry.

Cherry Bombe

(1999 Maraschino Cherry Contest Winner)

2 shots Stoli Vanil
2 shots Dr. McGillicuddy's vanilla schnapps
2 shots cherry juice
2 shots cream

Serve in a tall glass with a maraschino cherry tree.

Cherry Tree: Take one large drink straw and stick three maraschino cherries in stem first so they hang over the edge a bit.

Duke Mosakowski
New Hartford, NY

Cherry Bomber

1/2 oz. Captain Morgan
1/2 oz. Malibu rum
1/2 oz. Myers's rum
1/2 oz. blackberry brandy
1/2 oz. crème de banana
1 oz. orange juice
1/2 oz. cherry juice

Add three maraschino cherries. Blend with ice. Fill two straws with Bacardi 151. Load two maraschino cherries stem down in straws and enjoy.

Cherry Buster

1/2 oz. Tequila Rose
1/2 oz. white crème de cacao
1/2 oz. amaretto
3 maraschino cherries
splash maraschino cherry juice

Christine Merckle
Idaho Falls, ID

Cherry Buster II

1 oz. vodka
1 1/2 oz. cherry pucker
orange juice

Serve in a tall Tom Collins glass. Place an orange slice around a maraschino cherry for garnish.

Roger Maloney
Appleton, WI

Cherry Cheesecake A

1 part vanilla vodka
1 part cream
1 part amaretto
3 maraschino cherries per drink

D. Zimmerman
Duluth, MN

Cherry Cheesecake B

1 part Dr. McGillicuddy's vanilla
1 part cherry juice

Cherry Cheesecake with Chocolate

8 oz. vanilla ice cream
1 oz. cream cheese
splash of milk
2 diced maraschino cherries, stemless
1 1/2 shot cherry brandy
1 3/4 shot light crème de cacao

In a poco grande glass, pour cherry juice and chocolate syrup inside. Top with a pyramid of whipped cream, two straws, and two stemmed cherries as opposite straws.

Jay A. Welle
Moorhead, MN

Cherry Cream

1 oz. Bacardi light rum
1 oz. cream
1 oz. cherry liqueur

Cherry Daiquiri

1 1/2 oz. light rum
2 oz. prepared limeade
1/2 oz. sugar
1 oz. maraschino cherry juice
4–8 maraschino cherries

Garnish with a maraschino cherry.

Cherry Fish

1/2 oz. light rum
1/2 oz. ice
handful of Swedish Fish
3 maraschino cherries
1/2 oz. Rose's lime juice

Michael Arnold
Newport, RI

Cherry Flip

1 egg
6 oz. Danish cherry wine
2 tsp. sugar
1 tbs. lemon juice

Cherry Flurry

1/2 oz. white crème de cacao
3/4 oz. amaretto
1 1/2 oz. milk
1 oz. cherry juice
4 maraschino cherries
2 scoops vanilla ice cream

Nancy White
Texarkana, TX

Cherry Love

(1999 Maraschino Cherry Contest Winner)

1 1/3 oz. Bacardi light
1/2 oz. Cointreau
5 oz. maraschino cherries
2 scoops vanilla ice cream

Pour all ingredients into a blender with a little ice. Serve in a margarita glass. Garnish with a slice of lime and a maraschino cherry in center; place on top of the drink to create a flower.

Alberto Meza
Seattle, WA

Cherry Passion Potion

(1999 Maraschino Cherry Contest Winner)

1 1/2 oz. cherry juice
1 1/2 oz. passion fruit juice
1 oz. white rum

Blend. Serve in a rocks glass over ice garnished with the stem of a maraschino cherry dipped in dark chocolate.

Dolores Long
Van Nuys, CA

Cherry Piña

1 1/2 oz. light rum
1 1/2 oz. unsweetened pineapple juice
1 oz. Coco Lopez cream of coconut
1/2 oz. maraschino cherry juice
6–10 stemless and pitted maraschino cherries

Cherry Pop

(1999 Maraschino Cherry Contest Winner)

1 oz. Malibu rum
1/2 oz. peach schnapps
splash orange juice
5 cherries
splash maraschino cherry juice

Blend with one scoop of ice. Add a dollop of whipped cream and a maraschino cherry.

Mark Langell
Staten Island, NY

Cherry Repair Kit

1 oz. amaretto
1/2 oz. crème de cacao
1/2 oz. half-and-half
3 maraschino cherries
1/2 oz. maraschino cherry juice

Cherry Ripe

2 oz. gin
1 oz. Kirsch
1 oz. cherry brandy

Chevoney

1 oz. Galliano
1/2 oz. Grand Marnier
1/2 oz. vodka
1 scoop vanilla ice cream

Norbert F. Karch
Bailey's Harbor, WI

Chi Chi

1 1/2 oz. Absolut vodka
3/4 oz. pineapple juice
1 1/2 oz. Coco Lopez cream of coconut

Chicago Style

3/4 oz. Bacardi light rum
1/4 oz. Hiram Walker triple sec
1/4 oz. Hiram Walker anisette
1/4 oz. lemon or lime juice

Chi Chi

2 oz. Coco Lopez cream of coconut
2 oz. pineapple juice
1 1/2 oz. Finlandia vodka

Chip Shot

Equal parts:
  Kahlúa
  Irish cream
  half-and-half

Chiquita Punch

1 oz. banana liqueur
3/4 oz. orange juice
3/4 oz. heavy cream
1 tsp. grenadine
crushed ice

Garnish with a maraschino cherry.

Chiquita

1 1/2 oz. vodka
1/2 oz. banana liqueur
1/2 oz. lime juice
1/4 cup sliced bananas
1 tsp. orgeat syrup

Chocolada

2 oz. Bacardi light
1 1/2 oz. crème de coconut
1 1/2 oz. milk
1 oz. dark crème de cacao
1 cup ice

Garnish with whipped cream and chocolate chips.

Chocolate Almond Cream

1 cup vanilla ice cream
1/2 cup amaretto
1/2 cup crème de cacao

Chocolate Almond Kiss

1/2 oz. dark crème de cacao
1 oz. Frangelico
1/2 oz. Absolut vodka
6 oz. vanilla ice cream

Chocolate Black Russian

1 oz. Kahlúa
1/2 oz. vodka
2 scoops chocolate ice cream

Chocolate Cherry Bomb

1 1/2 oz. Godiva or Mozart chocolate
   liqueur
1 oz. half-and-half

*Blend with ice. Pour in a martini glass. Make a
pool of cherry juice in center; add a maraschino
cherry.*

Steven Lassoff
San Francisco, CA

Chocolate Cherry Chip Cocktail

1 oz. cherry brandy
1/4 oz. Kahlúa
1/4 oz. amaretto
1/2 oz. dark crème de cacao
2 oz. maraschino cherry juice

Blend with chocolate chip ice cream and dust with cocoa. Garnish with chocolate cherry bombs.

Chocolate Cherry Bombs: Soak a maraschino cherry in crème de cacao. Slit the maraschino cherry, stuff with chocolate chips, and dip in powdered sugar.

Jeff Markland & Sandi Bajorski
Kennebunkport, ME

Chocolate Colada

2 oz. rum
2 oz. Coco Lopez cream of coconut
2 oz. half-and-half
1 oz. chocolate syrup
1 cup ice

Chocolate Covered Strawberry

1/2 oz. Kahlúa
1 oz. rum
1/2 oz. triple sec
10 oz. strawberries

Chocolate Cream Dream

1 oz. Vandermint liqueur
1 oz. Irish cream liqueur
1/2 oz. Du Bouchette butterscotch schnapps
   liqueur
1 1/2–2 scoops vanilla ice cream

Chocolate Cream

3/4 oz. Bacardi gold rum
1/4 oz. Hiram Walker dark crème de cacao
1/4 oz. Hiram Walker white crème de menthe
1 oz. cream

Chocolate Kiss

3/4 oz. Hiram Walker Swiss chocolate
almond
3/4 oz. Hiram Walker spearmint schnapps
3/4 oz. Hiram Walker white crème de cacao

Chocolate Snow Bear

1 oz. amaretto
1 oz. crème de cacao
3 oz. chocolate ice cream
1/8 oz. chocolate syrup

Christmas Cranberry

1 1/2 oz. Finlandia cranberry vodka
1 1/2 oz. unsweetened pineapple juice
1 oz. Coco Lopez cream of coconut
6–10 pitted and stemless maraschino cherries

Cider Nectar

1 tsp. brandy
1 tsp. lemon juice
1 tsp. sugar

Fill with cider.

Citron Neon

1 1/2 oz. Absolut Citron
1/2 oz. Midori melon liqueur
1/2 oz. blue curacao
splash lime juice
1 oz. sweet & sour mix

Citrus Mist Colada

1 1/2 oz. Canadian Mist
4 1/2 oz. piña colada mix
2 oz. lemon-lime soda

Garnish with a maraschino cherry and lime.

Citrus Supreme

2 shots Gordon's citrus vodka
1 shot triple sec
1 12-oz. can frozen lemonade
2 cups lime or lemon-flavored water

Garnish with a slice of lemon.

Calm Voyage

1 oz. Bacardi light or dark rum
1/4 oz. apple brandy
1 oz. orange juice
dash Angostura bitters

Clover Cooler

1/2 oz. Baileys Irish cream
1/2 oz. Malibu rum
1/2 oz. blue curacao
4 oz. pineapple juice

Cockpit Cocktail

1 oz. Appleton gold Jamaican rum
1/2 oz. crème de cacao
1/2 oz. white crème de menthe
1 tbs. sweet cream
1 tsp. Appleton white rum

Coco Amadine

1 oz. almond liqueur
1 oz. Coco Lopez cream of coconut

Coco Colada

1 1/2 oz. dark crème de cacao
4 oz. pineapple juice
1 1/2 oz. Coco Lopez cream of coconut

*Garnish with a pineapple spear and a maraschino
cherry.*

Coco Dream

1 1/2 oz. white crème de cacao
1 1/2 oz. Coco Lopez cream of coconut
2 scoops vanilla ice cream
1/2 cup ice

Mix until smooth.

Courtesy of Bennigan's Restaurants, Inc.

Coco Java

1 oz. coffee liqueur
1 oz. Coco Lopez cream of coconut

Coco Loco (Crazy Coconut)

1 1/2 oz. tequila
3 oz. pineapple juice
2 oz. Coco Lopez cream of coconut

Garnish with a pineapple spear and a maraschino cherry.

Coco Lopez Limonade

3 oz. Coco Lopez lemonade mix
1 oz. Bacardi Limón

Coco Lopez Limon Madness

1/2 oz. Bacardi Limón
1/2 oz. Coco Lopez cream of coconut
1 oz. orange juice
1 oz. cranberry juice

Coco Lopez Purple Passion

1 1/2 oz. Bacardi light rum
3 oz. Coco Lopez Purple Passion colada mix

Cocobana

1 part Bacardi light
1 banana
1 part coconut milk

Susan McGowan
Oddfellows Restaurant

Coco-Mocha Alexander

1 1/2 oz. Irish cream liqueur
4 oz. Coco Lopez cream of coconut
2 oz. cold, black coffee

Mix until smooth.

Coco-Motion

1 1/2 oz. dark rum
4 oz. Coco Lopez cream of coconut
2 oz. lime juice

Coconut Banana Colada

2 oz. Cruzan coconut rum
3/4 oz. Cruzan banana rum
2 oz. Coco Lopez cream of coconut
3 oz. pineapple juice

Coconut Bellini

1/2 oz. peach schnapps
2 oz. Coco Lopez cream of coconut
2 oz. peach puree
3 oz. champagne

Blend first three ingredients. Top with champagne.

Coconut Bon Bon

2 oz. vodka
1 oz. Vandermint liqueur
2 oz. Coco Lopez cream of coconut
1 oz. half-and-half

Garnish with a maraschino cherry.

Coconut Colada

2 oz. Malibu rum
4 oz. Coco Lopez cream of coconut
2 oz. orange juice
1 oz. half-and-half

Coconut Daiquiri

1 1/2 oz. rum
1 1/2 oz. Coco Lopez cream of coconut
1/2 oz. lime juice

Coconut Grove

1 oz. rum
2 oz. Coco Lopez cream of coconut
1 oz. orange juice

Coconut Honey

1 oz. dark rum
2 oz. Coco Lopez cream of coconut
1 oz. honey

Coconut Punch

1 1/4 oz. Bacardi light rum
2 oz. Coco Lopez cream of coconut
1/4 oz. lemon juice
3-4 tbs. vanilla ice cream

Garnish with a maraschino cherry.

Coconut Punch

1 1/4 oz. Bacardi light or rum
2 oz. Coco Lopez cream of coconut
1/2 oz. lemon juice

Coconut Vodka Daiquiri or Chi Chi

1 oz. Finlandia vodka
2 oz. Coco Lopez cream of coconut
1/2 oz. lime juice
pineapple juice

Coffee Colada Freeze

1 oz. Kahlúa
1/2 oz. rum
1 oz. Coco Lopez cream of coconut
2 oz. pineapple juice

©2000 Vita-Mix Corporation

Coffee with Kirsch Cocktail
(Café Au Kirsch)

2 oz. Kirsch (or 1/2 Kirsch, 1/2 cognac)
2 oz. strong, cold coffee
1 egg white
1 1/2 tsp. sugar

Cointreau Colada

2 oz. Cointreau
2 oz. Coco Lopez cream of coconut
2 oz. pineapple juice

Cointreau Orange Freeze

2 oz. Cointreau
4 oz. orange soda
1 large scoop vanilla ice cream

Serve with an orange slice.

Cointreau Santa Fe Margarita

1 1/2 oz. Jose Cuervo gold tequila
3/4 oz. Cointreau
2 oz. sweet & sour mix
2 oz. cranberry juice

Cointreau Strawberry Margarita

1 1/4 oz. Jose Cuervo gold tequila
3/4 oz. Cointreau
2 oz. sweet & sour mix
3 oz. frozen strawberries

Cointreau-Band

2 oz. Cointreau
2 scoops chocolate ice cream

Garnish with a maraschino cherry.

Cold Orgasm

3/4 oz. Absolut vodka
3/4 oz. Kahlúa
3/4 oz. Baileys Irish cream

Garnish with a maraschino cherry.

Colonel's Collins

1 oz. gin
1 oz. Cointreau
1/2 lime, peeled

Garnish with an orange slice and a maraschino cherry.

Colorado Bulldog

1 1/4 oz. Kahlúa
4 oz. half-and-half

Blend and top with cola.

Columbia Cocktail

1 1/2 oz. Bacardi light or dark rum
1 oz. lemon juice
1 oz. raspberry syrup or several fresh or frozen
  raspberries

Comfort Colada

1 1/2 oz. Southern Comfort
1 oz. Coco Lopez cream of coconut
2 oz. pineapple juice

Garnish with a maraschino cherry.

Comfortable Freeze

1 oz. Southern Comfort
2 oz. pineapple juice
1/2 oz. grenadine

Garnish with a maraschino cherry.

Comfortable Watermelon

1 1/2 oz. Southern Comfort
1/2 oz. melon liqueur
1/2 oz. vodka
1 oz. cranberry juice
1 oz. pineapple juice

Comrade Coconut

1 oz. vodka
1/2 oz. white crème de cacao
3 oz. Coco Lopez cream of coconut

Continental Stinger

1 1/2 oz. vodka
3/4 oz. Hiram Walker peppermint schnapps

Continental

1 oz. Bacardi light rum
1/4 oz. green crème de menthe
3/4 oz. Rose's lime juice
1/4 tsp. sugar (optional)

Cool Banana

3/4 oz. Romana sambuca
3/4 oz. light rum
1 oz. lime juice
1/2 ripe banana
1 tsp. honey

Cool Irish Coffee Colada

1 oz. coffee liqueur
1 oz. Irish whiskey
1 1/2 oz. Coco Lopez cream of coconut
1 oz. cream

Cool Operator

3/4 oz. Midori melon liqueur
1/4 oz. vodka
1/4 oz. rum
splash lime juice
2 oz. grapefruit juice
2 oz. orange juice

Cool Southern Breeze

2 oz. Southern Comfort
1/2 oz. banana liqueur
1 oz. cranberry juice
1 oz. grapefruit juice
dash grenadine

Cooler

1 1/2 oz. Bacardi light rum
3/4 oz. lemon or lime juice
1/4–1/2 oz. white crème de menthe

Garnish with a sprig of mint.

Coral Cocktail

1 1/2 oz. Bacardi light rum
1/2 oz. apricot brandy
1/2 oz. lemon or lime juice
1/2 oz. grapefruit juice

Corn Popper Highball

2 oz. bourbon
1 tsp. grenadine
1 oz. cream
1 egg white

Cote Ce Cote La

1 1/2 oz. Bacardi white rum
1 1/2 oz. Coco Lopez cream of coconut
1/4 oz. fresh banana
1/2 oz. grenadine

*Garnish with orange slices and pineapple skin.
Serve with a fancy straw.*

Cotton Picker Cocktail

1 oz. Southern Comfort
1 oz. rum
1 oz. orange juice
1 oz. lemon juice

Cowboy's Punch

2 oz. Bacardi light or dark rum
1 oz. pineapple juice
1 oz. grapefruit juice
1 oz. lemon or lime juice

Coww Woww

1 1/2 oz. Bacardi light or dark rum
1 oz. lemon or lime juice
1 oz. cream

Cranberry Gin Sour

2 oz. gin
1/2 oz. triple sec
1 oz. lime juice or juice of 1/2 lime
1 oz. lemon juice or juice of 1/2 lemon
2 oz. light cream
1 tsp. sugar

Top with cranberry juice and club soda.

Cream de la CocoRibe

1/2 cup CocoRibe
1 cup vanilla ice cream
2 slices canned pineapple, drained

Cream Puff

1 1/2 oz. Bacardi light rum
2 oz. cream
1/2 oz. crème de noyaux (or almond liqueur)
1 egg white

Creamsicle Colada

2 oz. Bacardi spice
1/2 oz. triple sec
1/2 oz. white crème de menthe
2 oz. pineapple juice
1 oz. Coco Lopez cream of coconut
1 orange wheel

Garnish with an orange and pineapple wedge.

Jeannine Case
Oddfellows Restaurant

Creamy Screwdriver

2 oz. vodka
1 egg yolk
1/2 tsp. bar sugar
6 oz. fresh orange juice

Crème de Café

1 oz. bourbon
1 oz. cold water
1 oz. instant coffee
1 scoop vanilla ice cream

Garnish with a maraschino cherry.

Cricket

3/4 oz. Bacardi light rum
1/4 oz. white crème de cacao
1/4 oz. green crème de menthe
1 oz. cream

Garnish with a maraschino cherry.

Creamy Grasshopper

1 oz. white crème de cacao
1/2 oz. green crème de menthe
2 oz. vanilla ice cream

Garnish with a maraschino cherry.

Cruzan Frost

1 1/2 oz. Cruzan white rum
1/4 oz. white crème de menthe
1/2 oz. lemon sherbet

Garnish with a mint sprig.

Cuarenta y Tres Colada

1 oz. Licor 43
1/2 oz. dark rum
1 oz. Coco Lopez cream of coconut
2 oz. pineapple juice

Cuervo Acapulco Fizz

1 1/2 oz. Jose Cuervo gold tequila
1 1/2 oz. cream
2 oz. orange juice
3 ice cubes
2 tsp. granulated sugar
2 dashes orange bitters
1 whole egg

Garnish with an orange slice.

Cuervo Alexander

1 oz. Jose Cuervo gold tequila
1 oz. coffee liqueur
1 oz. wild cherry brandy
2 scoops vanilla ice cream

Garnish with a maraschino cherry.

Cuervo Gold Margarita

1 1/2 oz. Jose Cuervo gold tequila
1 oz. triple sec
2 oz. lime juice
2 oz. sweet & sour mix

Cuervo Raspberry Margarita

1 1/2 oz. Jose Cuervo gold tequila
1 oz. triple sec
1 oz. lime juice
1/2 cup raspberries, frozen
1/2 cup ice

Garnish with raspberries.

Cuervo Santa Fe Maggie

1 1/4 oz. Jose Cuervo gold tequila
1/2 oz. triple sec
2 oz. sweet & sour mix
2 oz. cranberry juice

Cuervo Strawberry Margarita

1 1/2 oz. Jose Cuervo gold tequila
1 oz. lime juice
1 oz. triple sec
1/2 cup frozen strawberries

Czar Mandarine

1 1/2 oz. Mandarine Napoleon
1 1/2 oz. cream
1 1/2 oz. vodka
dash grenadine

Garnish with an orange slice.

Czarina

1 oz. Stoli Razberi vodka
1 oz. Baileys Irish cream
1 oz. half-and-half or light cream
1 tsp. maraschino liqueur

Mix all the ingredients except the maraschino liqueur. Drip maraschino liqueur on top.

Daiquabu

1 1/2 oz. Malibu rum
1/2 oz. lime juice
1/4 oz. fruit of your choice

Daiquiri

1 1/2 oz. Canadian whisky
1/2 oz. light rum
1/2 oz. triple sec or Cointreau
2 oz. lemon/lime juice

Dark Canadian Colada

1 1/2 oz. Canadian whiskey
1/2 oz. dark crème de cacao
1 oz. Coco Lopez cream of coconut
2 oz. cream

Dark Mango Colada

1 oz. Bacardi dark rum
3 oz. Coco Lopez mango mix

Death by Chocolate

1 oz. vodka
1/2 oz. dark crème de cacao
1/2 oz. Baileys Irish cream
1 scoop vanilla ice cream

Deja Vu

1 1/4 oz. orange liqueur
1 oz. Coco Lopez cream of coconut
2 1/2 oz. orange juice
1/4 oz. orgeat syrup
1 cup ice

De-Minted De-Light

1 1/4 oz. Smirnoff vodka
1/2 oz. triple sec
2 oz. lime juice
1/2 oz. sugar in the raw
10 small mint leaves

Derby Daiquiri

1 oz. rum
1/2 oz. Cointreau
1 oz. orange juice
splash lime juice

Desert Cooler

1 1/2 oz. gin
1/2 oz. wild cherry brandy
1 oz. orange juice
1/2 oz. grenadine

Devil's Tail

1 1/2 oz. light rum
1 oz. vodka
2 tsp. apricot brandy
2 tsp. grenadine
1/2 oz. lime juice

Dirty Colada

1 1/2 oz. Bacardi black rum
2 oz. pineapple juice
1 oz. Coco Lopez cream of coconut

Garnish with a maraschino cherry.

Dirty Mutha

1 oz. coffee liqueur
1/2 oz. vodka
3 oz. chocolate ice cream

Garnish with a maraschino cherry.

Disarita Margarita

1 oz. Jose Cuervo 1800 tequila
1/2 oz. Disaronno amaretto
3 oz. margarita mix

Garnish with a lime.

Disaronno Dreamsicle

1 1/2 oz. Disaronno amaretto
2 oz. orange juice
2 oz. cream

Garnish with a maraschino cherry.

Disaronno Shortcake

1 oz. Disaronno amaretto
1 oz. Tuaca
2 oz. strawberries
3 oz. cream

Garnish with a maraschino cherry.

Disaronno Smoothie

2 oz. Disaronno amaretto
1 oz. sour mix
4–5 large strawberries

Garnish with a maraschino cherry.

Dixieland Special

2 oz. vodka
juice of 1/2 lime
watermelon chunks, seedless

Double Berry Coco Punch

20 oz. frozen strawberries in syrup,
  thawed
15 oz. Coco Lopez cream of coconut
48 oz. cranberry juice cocktail, chilled
2 cups light rum, optional
1 liter club soda, chilled

In a blender, puree the strawberries and cream of coconut until smooth. In a large punch bowl, combine the pureed mixture, cranberry juice, and rum (if desired). Just before serving, add club soda and serve over ice.

Dr. Root

1 1/2 oz. DeKuyper root beer schnapps
1 oz. Gilbey's light rum
4 oz. sweet & sour mix

Dreamsicle

1 part Cointreau
1 part cream
1 part orange juice
dash grenadine

Garnish with a maraschino cherry.

Dubonnet Fizz

2 oz. Dubonnet
1 tsp. cherry brandy
juice of 1/2 an orange
juice of 1/2 a lemon

Dubonnet Sour

1 oz. Dubonnet Rouge
2 oz. sweet & sour mix

Dynamic 'Rita

1 1/4 oz. Cuervo 1800 tequila
3/4 oz. Grand Marnier
2 oz. orange juice
1/4 oz. Rose's sweetened lime juice

Pour into a 16 oz. glass. Garnish with a lime slice.

Dyn-O-Mite Daiquiri

2 oz. rum
3 oz. orange banana liqueur
1/2 oz. triple sec
1 oz. lime juice

Egg Nog

8 oz. Vandermint liqueur
2 qts. eggnog
1 tbs. nutmeg
1 tbs. vanilla extract
cinnamon sticks

Egg Sour

2 oz. brandy
1 tsp. Cointreau
1/2 oz. lemon juice
1 egg

Eggnog Dot

1 oz. rum, brandy, whiskey, or sherry
5 oz. milk or milk and cream
1 egg
1 tsp. sugar

El Dorado

1 oz. Galliano
1/2 oz. white crème de cacao
3 oz. orange juice

Electric Lemonade

1 1/4 oz. vodka
1/2 oz. blue curacao
2 oz. sweet & sour mix
splash 7-Up

Garnish with a lemon slice.

Electric Peach

1 oz. vodka
1/4 oz. peach schnapps
1/2 oz. cranberry juice cocktail
1/4 oz. orange juice

Garnish with a lemon slice.

Emerald Isle

3/4 oz. Tullamore Dew
3/4 shot green crème de menthe
2 scoops vanilla ice cream

Top with a maraschino cherry.

Estate '85

1 oz. Galliano
1 oz. Mount Gay light rum
2 oz. lemon sherbet

Garnish with a sprig of mint and a wheel of kiwi to the side of the glass. Serve with straws.

Eve's Temptation

1 oz. Coco Lopez cream of coconut
1 1/4 oz. vodka
2 oz. apple juice
1 cup ice
cinnamon

Mix all ingredients except cinnamon in a blender until smooth. Sprinkle with cinnamon.

Eve's Apple

1 oz. apple-infused vodka
1/4 oz. Hot Damn! cinnamon schnapps
1/3 oz. blue curacao
1 1/2 oz. apple juice
1/3 oz. Angostura lime juice
1 cup vanilla ice cream
1 cup crushed ice

Garnish with a parfait apple and small orchid.

Evita Cocktail

1 oz. Midori melon liqueur
1 oz. Suntory vodka
1/2 oz. sweet & sour mix
1 1/2 oz. orange juice

Eye Opener

1 1/2 oz. Bacardi light rum
1/2 oz. anisette
1/4 oz. orange curacao
1/4 oz. white crème de cacao
1 egg yolk

Falling Leaves

1 oz. Gosling's Black Seal rum
1/2 oz. Marie Brizard raspberry liqueur
dash grenadine
4 oz. orange juice

Fern Gully

1 1/2 oz. Bacardi light rum
3/4 oz. Coco Lopez cream of coconut
1 oz. orange juice
1 oz. lemon or lime juice
1/4 oz. orgeat syrup

Finlandia Cranberry Cooler

2 oz. Finlandia cranberry
2 oz. Chambord
2 oz. cranberry juice

Finlandia Sea Goddess

2 oz. Finlandia Classic
1 oz. Alizé Passion liqueur
splash blue curacao

Fireman's Sour

1 1/2 oz. Bacardi light rum
1 1/2 oz. lemon or lime juice
1/2 tsp. sugar
1/4 oz. grenadine

Fill with club soda. Garnish with a maraschino cherry and a lemon or lime wheel.

First Cherry

1/2 oz. Bacardi 151
1/2 oz. cherry brandy
1/2 oz. Baileys Irish cream
1 oz. cream

Blend with 1 oz. cream, 3 shots maraschino cherry juice, and ice. Two maraschino cherries as garnish.

Cheryl Thorn
Duarte, CA

Flamingo

1 oz. Beefeater dry gin
2 oz. pineapple juice
1 oz. Coco Lopez cream of coconut
1 oz. Major Peters' sweet & sour mix

Florida Banana

1 1/4 oz. vodka
2 oz. Coco Lopez cream of coconut
4 oz. orange juice
1 medium banana

Floridita

1 1/2 oz. Bacardi light rum
1 oz. orange juice
1/2 oz. triple sec

Fluffy Duck

1 oz. gin
1 oz. advocaat
1/2 oz. Cointreau
1 oz. orange juice

Top with soda water. Garnish with a slice of orange and maraschino cherry.

Flying Grasshopper

1 oz. vodka
3/4 oz. green crème de menthe
3/4 oz. white crème de cacao
1 scoop vanilla ice cream

Flying Kangaroo

1 oz. Mount Gay rum
1 oz. vodka
1/4 oz. Galliano
1/4 oz. cream
1 1/2 oz. pineapple juice
3/4 oz. Coco Lopez cream of coconut
3/4 oz. orange juice

Foamy Orange Lime Cocktail

1/2 oz. orange juice
2 tbs. lime juice
1/2 cup white port
1 tbs. sugar
1 egg white

Forbidden Fruit

2 oz. Bacardi Select rum
1 oz. Bacardi dark rum
3 oz. passion fruit juice
2 oz. Coco Lopez cream of coconut
1/2 oz. shaved coconut

Mix Bacardi Select rum, passion fruit juice, Coco Lopez, and ice until thoroughly blended. Wet the rim of a tulip or hurricane glass and dip it in the shaved coconut until the entire rim is covered. Pour the blended mix into the glass until almost full. Pour the Bacardi dark rum over the top to make it float. Garnish with a maraschino cherry and serve.

Forbidden Fruit II

1 oz. vodka
1/2 oz. Bacardi
sweet & sour mix
cherry juice

Blend and float 151-proof rum. Garnish with a cherry.

Laura Hankins
Redding, CA

Forbidden Jungle

1 1/2 oz. rum
1/2 oz. peach schnapps
1 oz. Coco Lopez cream of coconut
1 1/2 oz. pineapple juice
1/4 oz. lime juice
dash grenadine

Foreign Affair

1 oz. Metaxa brandy
1/2 oz. Romana sambuca
juice of 1 lime

Forever Cherry

1 1/2 oz. Tropico rum
1/2 oz. Malibu rum
4 oz. cherry juice
1/2 oz. cream
5 maraschino cherries

Blend with ice to freeze. Serve in a balloon glass.
Garnish with a maraschino cherry.

Jimm Ramunnd
Painesville, OH

Frangelico Freeze

4 oz. vanilla ice cream
1 1/2 oz. Frangelico

Garnish with a maraschino cherry.

Freddie Fudpucker Freeze

1 1/2 oz. tequila
1/4 oz. Galliano
4 oz. orange juice

French Colada

1 1/2 oz. Puerto Rican white rum
3/4 oz. cognac
1 scoop crushed ice
3/4 oz. sweet cream
3/4 oz. Coco Lopez cream of coconut
1 1/2 oz. pineapple juice
splash crème de cassis

French Daiquiri

1 1/2 oz. Bacardi light rum
1/2 oz. Grand Marnier
3/4 oz. lemon or lime juice

French Dream

1/2 oz. Chambord
1 1/2 oz. Carolans Irish cream
2 oz. half-and-half
4 oz. ice cubes

Garnish with a maraschino cherry.

French Nipple

1 oz. Kahlúa
1 oz. amaretto
1 oz. vodka
1 scoop vanilla ice cream

Garnish with a maraschino cherry.

French Passion

2 oz. Passoã
1/2 oz. Rémy Martin cognac
3 oz. orange juice

Serve in a hurricane glass. Garnish with a half slice of orange on the rim.

Babe Loffredo
Jersey City, NJ

French Roulette

1 1/2 oz. vodka
1/2 oz. Mandarine Napoleon
3 oz. grapefruit juice

Garnish with a lime slice.

Frezsa Dorado

1 1/2 oz. Sauza Conmemorativo tequila
1/2 oz. Chambord
1/2 oz. peach puree
sweet & sour mix

Friar Tuck

1 oz. Kahlúa
3/4 oz. Frangelico
1/2 oz. cream

Garnish with a maraschino cherry.

Frosted Romance

1 oz. Chambord
1 oz. white crème de cacao
1 scoop vanilla ice cream

Garnish with a maraschino cherry.

Frosty Comfort

1 oz. Southern Comfort
1 cup orange juice
1 cup orange sherbet

Frosty Friar

1 1/2 oz. Frangelico liqueur
3/4 oz. white rum
1 scoop strawberry ice cream

Frozen Apple

1 1/2 oz. Laird's applejack
1 oz. lime juice
1 1/2 oz. sweet & sour mix
1/2 tsp. sugar

Frozen Apricot Sour

1 1/2 oz. apricot brandy
2 oz. orange juice
1 1/2 oz. prepared limeade
1 tsp. sugar

Frozen Aquavit

1 oz. Aquavit
1 oz. sweet & sour mix

Frozen Berkeley

2 oz. light rum
1/2 oz. brandy
1 tbs. passion fruit syrup
1 tbs. lime juice

Frozen California Sour

1 1/2 oz. bourbon
2 oz. orange juice
1 tsp. sugar

Frozen Fuzzy

3/4 oz. peach schnapps
1/4 oz. Cointreau
splash lime juice
splash grenadine
1 oz. lemon-lime soda

Frozen Golden

1 1/2 oz. Galliano
1/2 oz. white crème de cacao
3 oz. vanilla ice cream

Garnish with a maraschino cherry.

Frozen Hurricane

1 oz. light rum
1 oz. gold rum
1 oz. lime juice
1/4 oz. grenadine
1 oz. orange juice
1/2 oz. passion fruit syrup

Frozen Mexican Coffee

2 oz. Frangelico liqueur
1 1/2 oz. Coco Lopez cream of coconut
1 oz. chocolate syrup
4 oz. strong coffee

Frozen Mint Julep

2 oz. bourbon
1 oz. lemon juice
1 oz. sugar syrup
5-6 mint leaves

Frozen Peachy Orange Colada

1 1/2 oz. peach schnapps
2 oz. Coco Lopez cream of coconut
2 oz. orange juice
1/2 oz. grenadine

Frozen Pine

1 oz. Canadian Mist
2 oz. pineapple juice
1 oz. grenadine

Garnish with a maraschino cherry.

Frozen Pink Squirrel

1 oz. crème de noyaux
1/2 oz. white crème de cacao
3 oz. vanilla ice cream

Frozen Rhumba

1 1/2 oz. Bacardi light rum
2 oz. triple sec
1 oz. grapefruit juice
2 oz. orange juice
1/2 oz. lime juice

Frozen Scotch Sour

1 1/2 oz. scotch
2 oz. orange juice

Frozen Scotch

1 1/4 oz. scotch
1 oz. lemon juice
1 tsp. sugar

Fruit Salad

1 1/2 oz. DeKuyper Pucker Cheri-Beri
1/2 oz. DeKuyper Pucker grape
1/2 oz. Peachtree schnapps
splash orange juice

Funky Monkey

3/4 oz. rum
3/4 oz. white crème de cacao
3/4 oz. banana liqueur
1/2 fresh ripe banana, peeled

Garnish with a banana.

Funky Monkey II

1 oz. banana liqueur
2 oz. Kahlúa
1/2 oz. ice cream
1 oz. brandy

Garnish with a maraschino cherry.

Fuzzless Screwdriver

1 1/2 oz. Hiram Walker Jubilee peach
   schnapps
1 oz. vodka
2 oz. orange juice

Fuzzy Fruit

3/4 oz. peach schnapps
3/4 oz. amaretto liqueur
4 oz. orange juice
2 oz. peach nectar
2 oz. half-and-half

*Pour into a 16 oz. glass. Garnish with an orange
slice.*

Galliano Colada

3/4 oz. Galliano
3/4 oz. Mount Gay rum
2 oz. pineapple juice
1 oz. coconut milk

Garnish with a pineapple wedge and two maraschino cherries. Serve with straws.

Galliano Milkshake

2 oz. Galliano
8 oz. milk
2 generous scoops vanilla ice cream

Mrs. John Lockley
San Francisco, CA

Galliano Sunshine

1 1/4 oz. Galliano
1 scoop orange sherbet

Gaugin

2 oz. light rum
1 oz. passion fruit syrup
1 tsp. lime juice or juice of 1/2 lime
1 tsp. grenadine
1/2 tsp. fine sugar

Gay Galliano

1 1/2 oz. Mount Gay rum
3/4 oz. Galliano
1/2 oz. lime juice

Garnish with a slice of lime and a maraschino cherry.

Georgia Peach

1 1/2 oz. Bacardi light or dark rum
1/2 oz. peach brandy
3/4 oz. orange juice

Garnish with a peach slice.

German Peach

1 1/2 oz. vodka
1 oz. peach brandy
1 tsp. lemon juice
1 tsp. peach preserves
1 wedge canned or fresh peach cut

German Chocolate Cake

1/3 oz. Kahlúa
Layer:
   1/3 oz. Frangelico
   1/3 oz. crème de cacao
   1/4 oz. cream

Giada

1/2 oz. Galliano
3/4 oz. vodka
1/2 oz. Campari
1/4 oz. pineapple juice

Garnish with a maraschino cherry.

Gin Fizz

2 oz. dry gin
1 tbs. powdered sugar
juice of 1/2 lemon
juice of 1/2 lime

Blend and fill with carbonated water or seltzer.

Ginger Colada

1 1/2 oz. Canton Delicate ginger liqueur
1 1/2 tbs. Coco Lopez cream of coconut
1 oz. pineapple juice
1 oz. rum

Go Go Cherry Juice

1 oz. vodka
1 oz. maraschino cherry juice
3 oz. pineapple guava nectar
1 tbs. Coco Lopez cream of coconut

Garnish with three maraschino cherries.

Marily Ceccone
Westbury, NY

Godiva Irish Freeze

1 1/2 oz. Godiva liqueur
3/4 oz. Irish cream liqueur

Garnish with a maraschino cherry.

Godiva Whisper

3/4 oz. Godiva liqueur
1/2 oz. Martell cognac
3 scoops vanilla ice cream

Garnish with a maraschino cherry.

Golden Cadillac

2 oz. Galliano
1 oz. white crème de cacao
1 oz. half-and-half

Golden Chain

1 part Galliano
1 part Rémy Martin cognac
3/4 part fresh lime juice

Garnish with a slice of lime and maraschino cherry.

Golden Fizzer

2 oz. rum
1/2 lemon, peeled
1 tsp. sugar
1 egg yolk

Golden Gate

2 oz. gin or light rum
1/2 pint orange ice or sherbet

Golden Slipper

2 oz. apricot brandy
1 oz. yellow Chartreuse
1 egg yolk

Good and Plenty

1 oz. vodka
1 oz. coffee liqueur
dash Pernod
1/2 scoop vanilla ice cream

Good Fortune

1 oz. Canton Delicate ginger liqueur
1/2 oz. rum
1 1/2 oz. Devonshire cream liqueur
2 oz. vanilla ice cream

Garnish with three maraschino cherries.

Goombay Smash

1 oz. light rum
1 oz. dark rum
1 oz. Coco Lopez cream of coconut
1 oz. pineapple juice

Gorky Park Cooler

1 1/2 oz. Stoli Strasberi vodka
4 oz. pineapple juice
1/2 oz. spiced rum
1/2 oz. coconut rum

Grab My Coconuts

1 oz. Bacardi light
2 1/2 oz. Bartenders Good Time coconut rum
1 oz. pineapple juice

Tim Lowery, WI

Grand Finale

1 oz. hazelnut liqueur
1 oz. almond liqueur
2 oz. Coco Lopez cream of coconut
1 oz. light cream

Sprinkle with nutmeg.

Grand Marnier Margarita

1 oz. super premium tequila
1 oz. Grand Marnier
1 oz. fresh-squeezed lime juice
sugar to taste

Grapefruit Fizz

1 cup grapefruit juice
2 oz. sherry wine
1 egg white
1 tbs. sugar

Grasshopper

1 oz. white crème de cacao
1 oz. green crème de menthe
2 oz. whipping cream

Green Elevator
(Chartreuse Cocktail)

2 oz. green Chartreuse
juice of 1 lemon
2 tbs. grapefruit juice
1 egg white

Green Eyes

3/4 oz. Midori melon liqueur
1 oz. rum
1/2 oz. Coco Lopez cream of coconut
1/2 oz. Rose's lime juice
1 1/2 oz. pineapple juice

Groundhog's Shadow

2 oz. DeKuyper root beer schnapps
1 oz. Gilbey's gin
2 oz. light cream

Guava Colada

1 1/4 oz. vodka or rum
2 oz. guava nectar
1 1/2 oz. Coco Lopez cream of coconut

Guillotine

2 oz. Mandarine Napoleon
1/2 oz. white rum
1/2 oz. gin
1 oz. pineapple juice

Harbor Lights

1 oz. Puerto Rican rum
1 oz. tequila
1 oz. DeKuyper crème de cacao

Harvest Moon

1 oz. Mandarine Napoleon
2 oz. brandy
dash lemon juice

Garnish with a lemon twist.

Havana Banana Fizz

2 oz. light rum
2 1/2 oz. pineapple juice
1 1/2 oz. fresh lime juice
3-5 dashes Peychaud's bitters
1/3 banana, sliced
bitter lemon soda

Blend and fill with bitter lemon soda.

Havana Special

4 oz. white rum
1 tbs. maraschino liqueur
1/2 tbs. sugar
1 oz. lemon or lime juice

Hawaiian Daisy

1 1/2 oz. Bacardi light rum
1 oz. pineapple juice
1/4 oz. lemon or lime juice
1/4 oz. grenadine
1 egg white

Top with club soda.

Hawaiian Eye

1 1/2 oz. bourbon
1 oz. Kahlúa
1/2 oz. vodka
1/2 oz. banana liqueur
1 tsp. Pernod
1 oz. heavy cream

Garnish with a maraschino cherry and pineapple.

Hawaiian Holiday

1 1/2 oz. Bacardi light or dark rum
1 1/2 oz. guava juice
1 oz. grapefruit juice
dash bitters

Hawaiian Punch

3 oz. gin or rum
1 tsp. Grand Marnier
1 jigger lemon juice
2 tsp. sugar
3 oz. Coco Lopez cream of coconut

Garnish with a maraschino cherry and pineapple.

Hawaiian Sunset

1 oz. gin
1 1/2 oz. sweet & sour mix
3 oz. orange juice
dash grenadine

Garnish with an orange wedge and a maraschino cherry.

Heather's Dream

1/2 oz. Romana sambuca
1/2 oz. heavy cream
1/2 oz. canned peach or 1/2 ripe peach peeled

Garnish with a maraschino cherry.

Heavenly Ginger

1 oz. Canton Delicate ginger liqueur
1 oz. Devonshire cream liqueur

Hibiscus

1/2 oz. brandy or cognac
1/2 oz. Grand Marnier
1/2 oz. lemon juice
1/2 oz. lime juice
2 oz. orange juice

Ho Ho and a Barrel of Rum

1 1/2 oz. Hiram Walker Old Fashioned
   root beer schnapps
1 oz. rum
1 oz. milk or cream

Holiday Winter Mint

2/3 oz. Vandermint liqueur
2/3 oz. Du Bouchett green cream de menthe
2/3 oz. cream

Garnish with a maraschino cherry.

Honey Bee

1 1/2 oz. Bacardi light rum
3/4 oz. lemon or lime juice
3/4 oz. cream
3/4 oz. honey

Honeydew Daiquiri

1 oz. Midori melon liqueur
1/2 oz. white rum
1 oz. sweet and sour lemon

Honeysuckle Rose

1 1/2 oz. Bacardi dark rum
3/4 oz. lemon or lime juice
1/2 oz. honey
1/2 oz. grenadine

Honolulu Cocktail

1 1/2 oz. Bacardi light or dark rum
1 oz. pineapple juice
1 oz. lemon or lime juice
1 oz. orgeat syrup
1/2 oz. grenadine
dash bitters

Hop Scotch

3/4 oz. scotch
3/4 oz. blackberry brandy
1/4 oz. lemon juice
1 oz. Coco Lopez cream of coconut
1 1/2 oz. pineapple juice

Hot Dutch Hug

2 oz. Vandermint liqueur
1 oz. Du Bouchett crème de almond liqueur
1 oz. hot chocolate

Hot Lips

2 oz. Passoã
1/2 oz. tequila
2 oz. orange juice
1 oz. cranberry juice

Serve in a short tumbler glass. Garnish with a split strawberry and a split slice of orange on the rim.

Hot Rum Cow

2 oz. light rum
2 tsp. sugar
1/4 tsp. vanilla
1 oz. milk

Hummer

1 oz. Kahlúa
1/2 oz. rum
2 scoops vanilla or chocolate ice cream

Garnish with a maraschino cherry.

Hurrah Milk Punch

2 oz. whiskey
1/2 tsp. Jamaican rum
4 oz. milk
1 tsp. sugar syrup

Iceball

1 shot gin
1/2 shot white crème de menthe
1/2 shot sambuca
splash cream

Icebreaker

2 oz. tequila
1/2 oz. Cointreau
2 oz. grapefruit juice
3/4 oz. grenadine syrup

Ich Bien

2 oz. apple brandy
1/2 oz. white curacao
2 oz. half-and-half
1 egg yolk

Sprinkle with nutmeg.

Icy Brendan's

3 oz. Saint Brendan's Superior Irish
  cream
2 scoops vanilla ice cream

Garnish with a maraschino cherry.

Il Magnifico

1 oz. Tuaca
1 oz. Cointreau
1 oz. cream

Garnish with a maraschino cherry.

Illusion

1/2 oz. Midori melon liqueur
1/2 oz. vodka
1/2 oz. Cointreau
1 oz. Coco Lopez cream of coconut
2 oz. pineapple juice

In the Pink

1 1/4 oz. Myers's Original rum cream
1 oz. Coco Lopez cream of coconut
1 tsp. grenadine

International Cream

1/2 oz. Carolans Irish cream
1/2 oz. Kahlúa
splash Grand Marnier
2 scoops vanilla ice cream
splash milk

International Mai Tai

1/2 oz. Malibu rum
1/2 oz. Myers's dark rum
1/2 oz. rum
1 tsp. orgeat syrup
2 oz. pineapple juice
2 oz. sweet & sour mix

Irish Angel

1 oz. Bushmills Irish whiskey
1/4 oz. white crème de cacao
1/4 oz. white crème de menthe
1/2 oz. cream

Garnish with a maraschino cherry.

Irish Berry

1 oz. Irish cream liqueur
1/2 oz. vodka
1 oz. Coco Lopez cream of coconut
1 1/2 oz. strawberries
dash grenadine

Irish Dream

1/2 oz. Carolans Irish cream
1/2 oz. Hiram Walker hazelnut liqueur
1/2 oz. Hiram Walker dark crème de cacao
1 scoop vanilla ice cream

Garnish with a maraschino cherry.

Irish Eyes

1 oz. Irish whiskey
1/4 oz. green crème de menthe
2 oz. heavy cream

Garnish with a maraschino cherry.

Irish Fix

2 oz. Irish whiskey
1 oz. Irish Mist
1/2 oz. fresh lemon juice
1/2 oz. pineapple juice

Garnish with a lemon slice, orange slice, and pineapple spear.

Irish Kilt

1 oz. Irish whiskey
1 oz. scotch
1 oz. lemon juice
1 1/2 oz. sugar syrup or to taste
3–4 dashes orange bitters

Irish Lace

1 oz. Irish Mist
2 oz. Coco Lopez cream of coconut
2 oz. half-and-half
3 oz. pineapple juice

Garnish with an orange flag.

Irish Rainbow

1 1/2 oz. Irish whiskey
3–4 dashes Pernod
3–4 dashes orange curacao
3–4 dashes maraschino liqueur
3–4 dashes Angostura bitters

Twist an orange peel over drink and drop in.

Irish Raspberry

1 oz. Devonshire Irish cream
1/2 oz. Chambord

Irish Shillelagh

1 1/2 oz. Irish whiskey
1/2 oz. light rum
1/2 oz. sloe gin
1 tsp. powdered sugar
1 oz. lemon juice or juice of 1/2 lemon
1/4 cup peaches, fresh or canned, diced

Garnish with a few fresh raspberries.

Island Pleasure

1 oz. crème de banana
1/4 oz. Frangelico
2 oz. cream
1 1/2 oz. Angostura grenadine

Isle of Pines

2 oz. light rum
1/2 oz. fresh lime juice
1 tsp. peppermint schnapps
6 fresh mint leaves

Isle of the Blessed Coconut

2 oz. light rum
1/2 oz. fresh lemon juice
1/2 oz. fresh lime juice
1/2 oz. fresh orange juice
1 oz. Coco Lopez cream of coconut
1 tsp. orgeat syrup

Italian Alexander

3/4 oz. Disaronno amaretto
3/4 oz. white crème de cacao
2 oz. half-and-half
2 scoops vanilla ice cream

Dust with nutmeg.

Italian Banana

3/4 shot amaretto
3/4 shot crème de banana
2 oz. orange juice
1 oz. sweet & sour mix

Garnish with a cherry.

Italian Bushwacker

1/2 oz. Kahlúa
1/2 oz. Hiram Walker amaretto liqueur
1/2 oz. white rum
1/2 oz. Carolans Irish cream
2 oz. half-and-half

Garnish with a maraschino cherry.

Italian Colada

1 1/2 oz. Puerto Rican white rum
1/4 oz. amaretto
1/4 oz. Coco Lopez cream of coconut
3/4 oz. sweet cream
2 oz. pineapple juice

Italian Margarita

1 oz. Disaronno amaretto
1/2 oz. tequila
1/2 oz. triple sec
2 oz. sweet & sour mix

Italian Orange Blossom

1 1/2 oz. Galliano
1 oz. orange juice
dash tequila

Mrs. Sophia Dodge
Daly City, CA

Jack Rose

2 oz. applejack brandy
1 oz. lime or lemon juice
2 tbs. grenadine syrup
1 egg white

Jamaica Snow

2 oz. Appleton white rum
2 oz. Coco Lopez cream of coconut
1 1/4 oz. Rose's lime juice

Garnish with a lime wheel and crushed pineapple.

Jamaican Blues

1 1/4 oz. rum
1/2 oz. blue curacao
2 oz. Coco Lopez cream of coconut
2 oz. pineapple juice
2 cups ice

Jamaican Breeze

1 1/4 oz. Frangelico
3/4 oz. Bols ginger brandy
5 oz. pineapple juice
1/2 oz. Coco Lopez cream of coconut
1/2 oz. lime juice

Jamaican Shake

1 shot Myers's dark rum
1/2 shot blended whiskey
2 oz. milk or cream

Jelly Donut

1 1/4 oz. Disaronno amaretto
3/4 oz. Chambord
3 scoops raspberry sorbet
1/2 scoop vanilla ice cream

Jocko's Julep

3 oz. bourbon
1 oz. green crème de menthe
1 1/2 oz. fresh lime juice
1 tsp. bar sugar
5 fresh mint leaves

*Blend and top with sparkling water. Garnish with
a mint sprig.*

John Collins

2 oz. bourbon whiskey
1 tsp. sugar
1/2 lemon, peeled

Jungle Jim

2 oz. vodka
2 oz. crème de banana
2 oz. milk

Kahlúa Toreador

2 oz. brandy
1 oz. Kahlúa
1/2 egg white

Jungle Juice

1 1/2 oz. Jose Cuervo gold tequila
1 1/2 oz. pineapple juice
1 1/2 oz. cranberry juice
1 1/2 oz. freshly squeezed orange juice

Blend and top with lemon-lime soda.

Kahlúa and Cream or Milk

1 1/2 oz. Kahlúa
3 oz. milk

Kahlúa Banana Cream Fizz

2 oz. Kahlúa
1 oz. rum
1 banana, sliced
3/4 oz. lime juice
2 oz. half-and-half

Top with club soda.

Kahlúa Banana

1 1/2 oz. Kahlúa
3/4 oz. rum
2 oz. pineapple juice
2 oz. Coco Lopez cream of coconut
1 fresh banana

Kahlúa Blizzard

1 1/2 oz. Kahlúa
1 oz. white crème de menthe
4 oz. Coco Lopez cream of coconut

Garnish with whipped cream and shredded coconut.

Kahlúa Brandy Alexander

1 oz. Kahlúa
1 oz. brandy or cognac
2 large scoops vanilla ice cream

Kahlúa Cane

1 1/4 oz. Kahlúa
1/2 oz. peppermint schnapps
crushed candy cane

Kahlúa Cherry Fizz

1 1/2 oz. Kahlúa
1 1/2 oz. milk or cream

Blend and top with a splash of cherry cola. Garnish with a maraschino cherry.

Kahlúa Chi Chi

1 oz. Kahlúa
3/4 oz. vodka
2 oz. pineapple juice
1 oz. Coco Lopez cream of coconut

Kahlúa Chocolate Almond

1 1/2 oz. Kahlúa
3/4 oz. amaretto
1/2 oz. cream

Blend, splash cola, and top with a maraschino cherry.

Kahlúa Coconut Mudslide

1 oz. vodka
1/2 oz. Kahlúa
1/2 oz. Carolans Irish cream
1 oz. milk or cream
1 oz. Coco Lopez cream of coconut

Kahlúa Cognac & Cream

1 oz. Kahlúa
1/2 oz. cognac
2 oz. cream or milk

*Garnish with a dollop of whipped cream and a
cherry.*

Kahlúa Colada

1 1/2 oz. Kahlúa
1 oz. light rum
2 oz. Coco Lopez cream of coconut
2 oz. pineapple juice

Garnish with a maraschino cherry and pineapple.

Kahlúa Cream Soda

1 1/2 oz. Kahlúa
2 oz. cream

*Blend and top with club soda and a maraschino
cherry in a tall glass.*

Kahlúa Creamsicle

1 1/2 oz. Kahlúa
orange juice
milk or cream

Garnish with a slice of orange.

Kahlúa Dublin Banana

1 oz. Kahlúa
1 oz. Irish cream
1/2 oz. half-and-half
banana

Garnish with a banana sliver.

Kahlúa Fuzz Buster

1 1/2 oz. Kahlúa
1/2 oz. peach schnapps
1 oz. cream
1 oz. soda

Garnish with a slice of peach. Top with club soda.

Kahlúa Kialoa

1 1/2 oz. Kahlúa
1 1/2 oz. dark rum
1 oz. cream

Kahlúa Mudslide

1/2 oz. Kahlúa
1/2 oz. Irish cream liqueur
1 oz. vodka
1 oz. milk or cream

Kahlúa Peanut Butter Cocktail

1 1/2 oz. Kahlúa
1/2 oz. tequila
1 1/2 oz. cream
1 tbs. creamy peanut butter

Kahlúa Peppermint Patty

1 oz. Kahlúa
1/2 oz. white crème de menthe
vanilla ice cream

Garnish with a mint leaf.

Kahlúa Polar Bear

1 oz. Kahlúa
1 oz. vodka
2 scoops vanilla ice cream

Kahlúa Stinger

1 3/4 oz. Kahlúa
3/4 oz. white crème de menthe

Kahlúa Strawberries & Cream

1 1/2 oz. Kahlúa
1 oz. strawberry schnapps
fill half-and-half

Garnish with a strawberry.

Kahlúa Strawberry Colada

1 1/2 oz. Kahlúa
1 oz. light rum
1 oz. Coco Lopez cream of coconut
2 oz. pineapple juice
fresh strawberries or 4 oz. strawberry schnapps

Garnish with a strawberry or pineapple wedge.

Kahlúa Strawberry Cream Daiquiri

1 1/2 oz. Kahlúa
1/2 oz. rum
1/2 oz. lime juice
4 medium, ripe strawberries
1 oz. half-and-half

Garnish with a strawberry.

Kahlúa Toasted Almond

1 oz. Kahlúa
1/2 oz. Disaronno amaretto
2 oz. cream or milk

Kahlúa Top Banana

1 1/2 oz. Kahlúa
1 oz. crème de banana
2 oz. milk or cream

Kahlúa White

1 oz. Kahlúa
1/2 oz. light rum
2 oz. milk or cream

Kalada

1 oz. Kahlúa
1/2 oz. Myers's rum
2 oz. pineapple juice
1 oz. Coco Lopez cream of coconut

Karamozov Koffee

1 oz. Stoli Kafya vodka
1 oz. Disaronno amaretto
1 oz. white crème de cacao

Key Largo

2 oz. dark rum
1 oz. Coco Lopez cream of coconut
1 scoop orange sherbet

Garnish with an orange.

Key Lime Dream

1 1/2 oz. light rum
3/4 oz. Rose's lime juice
2 scoops vanilla ice cream

Key West Freeze

1 1/4 oz. Frangelico
1/4 oz. Bols blue curacao
1 1/2 oz. Coco Lopez cream of coconut
3/4 oz. sweetened lime juice
2 oz. orange juice

Killer Colada

3 oz. Whaler's Killer coconut rum
3 tbs. coconut milk
3 tbs. pineapple, crushed
2 cups crushed ice

Serve with a pineapple wedge.

King Alexander

1 oz. gin
1 oz. white crème de cacao
1 oz. vanilla ice cream

Garnish with freshly grated nutmeg.

Kingston Combo

2 oz. Appleton dark Jamaican rum
4 oz. pineapple juice
1/2 oz. lime juice

Garnish with a maraschino cherry or pineapple spear.

Kingston

1 oz. Appleton Jamaican rum
1/2 oz. Tanqueray gin
juice of 1/2 lime or lemon
1 tsp. grenadine

Kiss o' the Nile

2 oz. gin
1/2 pint lemon-lime sherbet

Garnish with a mint leaf.

Kocktail Kid

1 oz. Captain Morgan rum
1/2 oz. triple sec
1 oz. maraschino cherry juice
1 oz. sweet & sour mix
1 oz. pineapple juice

Blend with ice. Serve in a martini glass.

Mohsen Alam El Din
Mt. Kisco, NY

Kremlin Cocktail

2 oz. vodka
1 1/2 oz. white crème de cacao
1 1/2 oz. half-and-half

La Bamba Margarita

1 1/4 oz. Sauza Conmemorativo tequila
1/2 oz. Hiram Walker triple sec
1/4 oz. grenadine
1/4 oz. pineapple juice
1 1/2 oz. orange juice

Garnish with a pineapple.

La Bamba

1 oz. Sauza extra gold
1/2 oz. Frangelico
1 1/2 oz. banana
3 oz. orange juice

Blend and add a splash of 7-Up.

La Dolce Vita

1 1/2 oz. Hiram Walker sambuca
3 oz. coffee ice cream

Garnish with a maraschino cherry.

La Florida

4 oz. white rum
2 oz. curacao
1 tbs. orange juice
2 tsp. sugar
1 oz. lemon or lime juice

La Vie En Rose

1 oz. gin
1 oz. Kirsch
1 oz. lemon juice
1/2 oz. grenadine

Labadu

3 oz. Malibu rum
3 oz. pineapple juice
1 oz. milk or vanilla ice cream

Lady Luck

1/2 oz. Hiram Walker blackberry brandy
1/2 oz. Hiram Walker amaretto
1/2 oz. Hiram Walker sambuca
2 oz. cream

Garnish with a maraschino cherry.

Latin Love

1 1/2 oz. Jose Cuervo Especial tequila
1 oz. Disaronno amaretto
1/2 can (6 oz.) Coco Lopez cream of coconut

Garnish with an orange or lemon. Serve in a bell glass with a sugared rim dipped in amaretto.

Lava Flow

1 1/4 oz. light rum
1/2 banana
2 oz. colada mix (pineapple juice and coconut
   syrup)
1 oz. liquid ice cream
1/4 cup strawberry puree

*Blend rum, banana, colada mix, and ice cream.
Pour strawberry puree into a glass about 1/8
full, then pour blended mixture over the top to
create a swirl.*

Lava Glow

1 oz. sloe gin
2 oz. ginger ale
1 oz. orange juice
4 cherries
crushed ice

*Blend and add ginger ale. Serve in a cordial glass
topped with whipped cream and a cherry.*

Rose Muzika
Uniontown, PA

Lazzaroni French Connection

1 part Lazzaroni amaretto
2 parts Ansac cognac

Lazzaroni Frost

1 1/2 oz. Lazzaroni amaretto
1/2 cup plain yogurt
1 oz. coconut cream
2 oz. orange juice

Leprechaun

2 oz. Irish whiskey
1 oz. light rum
1/2 oz. sloe gin
1 oz. fresh lemon juice
1/2 tsp. bar sugar
1/4 fresh peach, peeled and diced

Garnish with fresh raspberries.

Leprechaun's Libation

2 1/2 oz. Bushmills Irish whiskey
1/2 oz. green crème de menthe

Licorice Mist

1 1/2 oz. Romana sambuca
2 oz. Coco Lopez cream of coconut
2 oz. half-and-half

Licorice with a Twist

1 1/2 oz. Hiram Walker licorice schnapps
3 oz. coffee ice cream

Lifesaver

1 oz. Smirnoff vodka
1 oz. triple sec
2 oz. orange juice
2 oz. pineapple juice
1/2 tsp. grenadine

Lighthouse Laddie

1 oz. rum
1 oz. dark crème de cacao
1/2 oz. butterscotch schnapps
2 oz. Coco Lopez cream of coconut
2 oz. half-and-half

Lime Daiquiri

1 1/4 oz. rum
4 oz. sweet & sour mix
juice 1/2 fresh lime

Garnish with a lime wheel.

©2000 Vita-Mix Corporation

Limey

2 oz. light rum
1/2 oz. triple sec
1 tbs. lime juice

Garnish with a lime slice.

Lipshitz Libation

1 1/2 oz. Puerto Rican rum
1 oz. Disaronno amaretto
3 oz. half-and-half

Blend with ice and serve.

London Fog

1 oz. white crème de menthe
1 oz. Pernod
1 scoop vanilla ice cream

Long Stemmed Rose

1 1/2 oz. Tequila Rose
1 oz. Nestlé Quik strawberry syrup
1 large scoop strawberry ice cream
4 maraschino cherries, stemless
1 large scoop ice
1/2 cup whole milk

Pour into a hurricane glass. To create the rose stem garnish: whipped cream and two maraschino cherries.

Jeanne Marie Gendreau
Owasso, OK

Louisiana Lady

1 1/2 oz. Bacardi light rum
3/4 oz. lemon or lime juice
1/2 tsp. sugar
1 egg white
dash Peychaud's bitters

Love Potion

1 oz. rum
1/2 oz. banana liqueur
1/2 oz. triple sec
1 oz. orange juice
1 oz. pineapple juice

Garnish with orange, pineapple, and banana.

Lt. Kije's Kolada

1 1/2 oz. Stoli Strasberi vodka
1/2 oz. light rum
1/2 oz. small ripe banana
1/4 cup fresh strawberries
3 oz. pineapple juice
1 oz. Coco Lopez cream of coconut

Lucky Irish

1 1/2 oz. Irish whiskey
1/2 oz. sloe gin
1/2 oz. light rum
1 oz. Angostura lime juice
1/2 oz. Angostura grenadine

Garnish with two peach slices (diced), five to six fresh raspberries, and one maraschino cherry.

Lucky Lady

3/4 oz. Bacardi light-dry rum
1/4 oz. Romana sambuca
1/4 oz. Hiram Walker white crème de cacao
3/4 oz. cream

Garnish with a maraschino cherry.

Magpie

1 oz. vodka
1/2 oz. white crème de cacao
1 oz. Midori melon liqueur
3/4 oz. cream

Garnish with a maraschino cherry.

Mahogany Mauler

1 oz. vodka
1 oz. cherry brandy
1 oz. orange juice

Mahukona

2 oz. light rum
1/2 oz. white curacao
1/2 oz. fresh lemon juice
1/2 tsp. almond syrup
5 dashes orange bitters

Garnish with a pineapple spear.

Mai Tai

1 1/4 oz. Malibu rum
3/4 oz. dark rum
3 oz. pineapple juice
1 oz. sweet & sour mix

Garnish with a pineapple flag.

©2000 Vita-Mix Corporation

Major Margarita

1 1/2 oz. Jose Cuervo tequila
1/2 oz. Major Peters' lime juice
4 oz. Major Peters' margarita mix

Major Strawberry Margarita

1 1/2 oz. Jose Cuervo tequila
1/2 oz. Major Peters' lime juice
1/2 cup strawberries (fresh or frozen) or 4 oz.
   Major Peters' strawberry margarita mix

Malibu California Coastline

1 oz. Malibu rum
1 oz. peach schnapps
1/2 oz. blue curacao
2 oz. sweet & sour mix
2 oz. pineapple juice

Garnish with a pineapple wedge.

Malibu Caribbean Cooker

2 oz. Malibu rum
1/2 ripe banana
1/2 scoop vanilla ice cream

Malibu Coconut Colada

2 oz. Malibu rum
4 oz. Coco Lopez cream of coconut
2 oz. orange juice
1 oz. half-and-half

Top with toasted coconut.

Malibu Conga Punch

3 oz. Malibu rum
2 oz. pineapple juice
2 oz. orange juice
2 oz. grapefruit juice
dash bitters

Malibu Mai Tai

1/2 oz. Malibu rum
1/2 oz. Myers's dark rum
1/2 oz. rum
2 oz. pineapple juice
2 oz. sweet & sour mix

Malibu Margarita

1 1/2 oz. Malibu rum
1 oz. Cointreau
2 oz. lime juice

Malibu Orange Colada

1 1/2 oz. Malibu rum
1 oz. triple sec
3 oz. Coco Lopez cream of coconut

Malibu Shake

1 1/2 oz. Malibu rum
1 oz. white crème de menthe
3 oz. pineapple juice
2 oz. cream

Malibu Slide

Equal parts:
  Baileys Irish cream
  Kahlúa
  Malibu rum

Malibu Smooth Grove

1 1/2 oz. Malibu rum
1 1/2 oz. Midori melon liqueur
1 1/2 oz. Baileys Irish cream
1 scoop vanilla ice cream

Malibu Sunset

1 1/2 oz. Malibu rum
2–3 oz. strawberries
1 oz. pineapple juice
2 oz. orange juice
splash cream

Garnish with a maraschino cherry.

Malibu Tropicale

1 oz. Malibu rum
1/2 oz. Midori melon liqueur
3/4 oz. crème de banana
2 oz. pineapple juice
2 oz. papaya juice

Mandarinella

1 oz. Mandarine Napoleon
3 oz. Rémy Martin cognac
1 tsp. cream

Mango Sunset

In 23 oz. hurricane glass, place 4 level
  scoops of mango sorbet (sorbet size
  scoop). Fill glass with small ice cubes
  within 2 inches from the rim. Add:
4 oz. lemon sour collins mix (liquid form)
4 oz. orange juice
1 1/2 oz. milk or cream
dollop grenadine
2 oz. Bacardi white rum

*Pour into a hurricane glass. Top off with 7-Up or
Sprite. Garnish with a sprig of mint leaf.*

Eddie Doyle
Bull & Finch Pub
Boston, MA

Maraschino Cherry

3/4 shot rum
1/4 shot amaretto
1/4 shot peach schnapps
1 oz. cranberry juice
1 oz. pineapple juice
splash grenadine
whipped cream
1 maraschino cherry

Margarita Madness

1 1/2 oz. tequila
1/2 oz. triple sec
3 oz. Coco Lopez margarita mix

Margarita Madres

1 1/4 oz. Jose Cuervo gold tequila
1/2 oz. Cointreau
1 1/2 oz. sweet & sour mix
1 1/2 oz. orange juice
1 1/2 oz. cranberry juice

Garnish with a lime and maraschino cherry.

Margarita

1 oz. tequila
1 oz. Cointreau
1 oz. sweet & sour mix or lime juice

Garnish with a lime wheel.

Martha's Melons

1 oz. Midori melon liqueur
1 oz. Puerto Rican rum
2 oz. lemon mix
slice watermelon
slice cantaloupe
slice honeydew melon

Mary Rose

1 oz. cherry brandy
1 oz. gin
1/2 oz. port wine

Matador

1 oz. tequila
2 oz. pineapple juice
2 tsp. lime juice

Maui Breeze

1/2 oz. amaretto
1/2 oz. Cointreau
1/2 oz. brandy
1 oz. lemon juice or juice of 1/2 lemon
1 tsp. fine sugar
2 oz. pineapple juice
2 oz. guava juice

Maui Fizz

1 oz. light rum
1/3 oz. dry sherry
splash sweet cream

Garnish with an orange slice and a maraschino cherry.

Mello Mint

1 oz. Vandermint liqueur
1/2 oz. Du Bouchett melon liqueur
1/2 oz. Lazzaroni amaretto

Melon Colada

1 oz. rum
1/4 oz. Midori melon liqueur
2 oz. pineapple juice
3 oz. Coco Lopez cream of coconut
splash cream

Garnish with a maraschino cherry.

Melon Colada

1 oz. light rum
1 oz. Midori melon liqueur
2 oz. Coco Lopez cream of coconut
4 oz. pineapple juice

Garnish with a maraschino cherry.

Melon Cooler

2 oz. white wine
4 oz. fresh melon (any kind)
1/2 oz. Rose's lime juice
1/2 oz. Rose's grenadine

Melonhopper

1 oz. Midori melon liqueur
1/2 oz. white crème de cacao
1/2 oz. cream

Metaxa Olympic Cocktail

3/4 oz. Metaxa brandy
1/2 oz. Cointreau
3 oz. orange juice

Garnish with a maraschino cherry.

Mexican Mist

1 1/2 oz. Sauza Conmemorativo tequila
Equal parts: pineapple, orange, and cranberry
  juice

Mexican Pain Killer

1/2 oz. gold tequila
1/2 oz. vodka
1/2 oz. light rum
1 oz. pineapple juice
1/2 oz. orange juice
2 tbs. Coco Lopez cream of coconut

Garnish with a maraschino cherry.

Mexican Storm Cloud

2 oz. DeKuyper root beer schnapps
2 oz. Sauza tequila
1 oz. lime juice

Miami Fizz

1 1/2 oz. Bacardi light or dark rum
1 oz. lemon juice
1/4 oz. grenadine
1/4 tsp. sugar
1 egg white

Blend and top with club soda.

Miami Ice

3/4 oz. rum
3/4 oz. peach schnapps
1/2 oz. Coco Lopez cream of coconut
3 oz. pineapple juice
1/4 oz. grenadine

Blend and top with club soda.

Miami Special

1 oz. Bacardi light-dry rum
1/4 oz. Hiram Walker white crème de menthe
3/4 oz. lime juice

Midnight Orchid

1 1/2 oz. Finlandia cranberry vodka,
  chilled
1/4 oz. Chambord
2 oz. pineapple juice
1/2 oz. half-and-half

Garnish with a maraschino cherry.

Midori Alexander

1 1/2 oz. Midori melon liqueur
1 oz. brandy
1 oz. cream

Garnish with a maraschino cherry.

Midori Cheap Shades

1 3/4 oz. Midori melon liqueur
3/4 oz. peach schnapps
2 oz. orange juice
2 oz. pineapple juice
1 oz. margarita mix

Top with lemon-lime soda.

Midori Colada

1 oz. Midori melon liqueur
1/2 oz. Bacardi rum
2 oz. Coco Lopez cream of coconut
1 1/2 oz. pineapple juice

Garnish with a maraschino cherry and an orange.

Midori Daiquiri

1 oz. Midori melon liqueur
1/2 oz. white rum
1 oz. sweet & sour mix

Garnish with a maraschino cherry.

Midori Eggnog

1 oz. Midori melon liqueur
2 oz. eggnog

Top with nutmeg.

Midori Frozen Melonball

2 oz. Midori melon liqueur
1 oz. vodka (optional)
4 oz. orange, pineapple, or grapefruit juice

Midori Frozen Sour

1 oz. Midori melon liqueur
2 oz. sweet & sour mix

Garnish with a maraschino cherry and an orange slice.

Midori Green Iguana Margarita

1/2 oz. Midori melon liqueur
1 oz. tequila
2 oz. sweet & sour mix

Midori Hopper

1 oz. Midori melon liqueur
1/2 oz. white crème de menthe

Midori Magic

2 oz. Midori melon liqueur
1/2 oz. Cointreau
2 oz. cream

Garnish with a maraschino cherry.

Midori Margarita

1 1/2 oz. tequila
1 oz. Midori melon liqueur
1 oz. sweet & sour mix

Midori Sour

1 oz. Midori melon liqueur
2 oz. sweet & sour mix

Milky Way

1 oz. Cointreau
1/2 oz. dark crème de cacao
cream

Top with whipped cream and a maraschino cherry.

Mint 'N Cream

1 1/2 oz. Hiram Walker spearmint
  schnapps
3 oz. vanilla ice cream

Garnish with a maraschino cherry.

Mint Cocktail

1 1/2 jiggers gin
1/2 jigger green crème de menthe
2 jiggers dry white wine
2 sprigs fresh mint

Mint Condition

3/4 oz. vodka
1/2 oz. Kahlúa
3/4 oz. bourbon
3/4 oz. peppermint schnapps
3 oz. vanilla ice cream

Garnish with a maraschino cherry.

Mint Daiquiri

2 1/2 oz. light rum
2 oz. lime juice
1 tsp. sugar
6 mint leaves

Mint Julep (Blender Style)

3 mint sprigs, plus 2 for garnish
dash water
2 tsp. confectioners' sugar
2 oz. Makers Mark bourbon

Place three mint sprigs, water, and 1 teaspoon of sugar in a blender. Blend thoroughly. Add 1 cup crushed ice and bourbon. Blend a few seconds more. Pour into frosted glasses filled with crushed ice. Garnish with mint sprigs. Sprinkle remaining confectioners' sugar on top. Serve with a straw.

Mississippi Mud

1 1/2 oz. Southern Comfort
1 1/2 oz. coffee liqueur
2 large scoops vanilla ice cream

Garnish with a maraschino cherry.

Mist Cream

1 1/2 oz. Canadian Mist
1 cup ice
1/2 cup heavy cream
1/2 oz. coffee liqueur
dash grenadine

Garnish with a maraschino cherry.

Mistral

1 oz. Chambord
2 oz. dry white wine
1 tbs. frozen strawberries or raspberries

Monkey Special

1 oz. dark rum
1 oz. light rum
1/2 oz. banana, peeled
2 oz. vanilla or chocolate ice cream

Sprinkle with shaved chocolate.

Mont Blanc

1 oz. Chambord
1 oz. Absolut vodka
1 oz. cream or half-and-half
1 scoop vanilla ice cream

Garnish with a maraschino cherry.

Montego Margarita

1 1/2 oz. Appleton Estate rum
1/2 oz. triple sec
1 oz. lemon or lime juice
1 scoop crushed ice

Montezuma

2 oz. gold tequila
1 oz. madeira wine
1 egg yolk

Montmarte Special

1 1/2 oz. Bacardi light rum
3/4 oz. cream
1/4 oz. grenadine

Sprinkle nutmeg on top.

Montmartre

1 oz. Chambord
1 oz. Hiram Walker coffee liqueur
1 oz. cream or half-and-half

Garnish with a maraschino cherry.

Moonlight

1 oz. Canton Delicate ginger liqueur
1 oz. dark crème de cacao
1 oz. heavy cream

Garnish with a maraschino cherry.

Morgan Cannonball

1 1/4 oz. Captain Morgan spiced rum
3 oz. pineapple juice

Float white crème de menthe.

Morgan Spiced Cream

2 oz. Captain Morgan spiced rum
2 egg yolks
1 tsp. superfine sugar
2 oz. heavy cream, whipped stiffly

Garnish with a maraschino cherry.

Morning Glory Daisy

2 tsp. Pernod
2 oz. gin, brandy, or whiskey
1/2 egg white
1 tsp. bar sugar

Blend top with club soda.

Morning Glory

2 oz. gin
juice of 1 lime
1 egg
4 tsp. green crème de menthe

Morning Midori

1 oz. Midori melon liqueur
2 oz. orange juice
1/2 oz. cream

Garnish with a maraschino cherry.

Moscow Mimosa

1 1/2 oz. vodka
3 oz. orange juice, chilled

Blend, then top with champagne.

Mozart Maraschino Struzzel Sip

1 oz. Frangelico
1/3 oz. Goldschlager
dash cherry juice
1 oz. cream or milk

Blend with ice and garnish with a cherry.

Nicola Sweet
Fort Pierce, FL

Myers's Banana Daiquiri

1 1/2 oz. Myers's rum
1/2 oz. lemon juice
1/2 sliced ripe banana
1 tsp. sugar

Myers's Orange Daiquiri

1 1/2 oz. Myers's rum
1 oz. orange juice
1/2 oz. lime juice
1 tsp. sugar

Myers's Peach Daiquiri

2 oz. Myers's rum
2 fresh, peeled peach halves
1 tsp. sugar
1 oz. lime or lemon juice

Myers's Piña Colada

1 1/4 oz. Myers's Original dark rum
1 oz. Coco Lopez cream of coconut
2 oz. pineapple juice
2 oz. orange juice

Garnish with a maraschino cherry.

Myers's Pineapple Daiquiri

2 oz. Myers's rum
1/2 slice of canned pineapple
1 tbs. lime juice
1 tsp. sugar

Garnish with a maraschino cherry.

Myers's Rum Cream Dream

1 1/4 oz. Myers's Original rum cream
1 oz. Coco Lopez cream of coconut
1/2 oz. chocolate syrup

Myers's Strawberry Daiquiri

1 1/4 oz. Myers's dark rum
1/2 oz. Cointreau
juice of 1/2 lime
1/2 cup strawberries
1 tsp. bar sugar

Neopolitan

1 1/2 oz. Bacardi light or dark rum
1/2 oz. triple sec
1/2 oz. Grand Marnier
1/2 oz. lemon or lime juice

Nevada Cocktail

1 1/2 oz. Bacardi light rum
3/4 oz. grapefruit juice
1/2 oz. lemon or lime juice
dash bitters
1/2 tsp. sugar

New Orleans Night

1 oz. praline liqueur
1 oz. vodka
2 oz. Coco Lopez cream of coconut
1 oz. half-and-half

Garnish with a maraschino cherry.

New York White Colada

4 oz. New York white table wine
1/4 oz. fresh or canned pineapple with juice
1/2 scoop pineapple sherbet
1 cup ice cubes

Blend until smooth. Garnish with a pineapple wedge and white grapes.

©2000 Vita-Mix Corporation

New Yorker Highball

2 oz. bourbon
1 tsp. lemon juice
1 tsp. sugar syrup

Blend. Fill with carbonated water or soda; float 1 oz. Claret on top.

Nuclear Reactor

1 1/2 oz. Smirnoff vodka
1/2 oz. Bacardi light rum
1/2 oz. Malibu rum
1/2 oz. Coco Lopez cream of coconut

Nut and Honey

1 1/2 oz. vodka
3/4 oz. Frangelico
2 tbs. honey
3 oz. vanilla ice cream

Garnish with a maraschino cherry.

Nutty Buddie

1/2 oz. Frangelico
1/2 oz. butterscotch schnapps
1/2 oz. Kahlúa
1/2 oz. Baileys Irish cream
1/2 oz. milk

Garnish with a maraschino cherry.

Gina Geremia
Jeanie Ryan's Cafe
Branford, CT

Nutty Colada

1 oz. Frangelico
1 oz. rum
2 oz. Coco Lopez cream of coconut
1/2 cup fresh or canned pineapple

Garnish with pineapple, maraschino cherry, and shaved almonds.

Nutty Colada II

2 oz. amaretto
1 oz. gold rum
1 oz. coconut milk
1 tbs. coconut syrup
2 oz. pineapple juice
1/4 tsp. crème de noyaux

Garnish with a pineapple spear and a maraschino cherry.

Nutty Colada Easy

2 oz. amaretto
2 oz. Coco Lopez cream of coconut
3 oz. pineapple juice

Garnish with a maraschino cherry.

Nutty Squeeze

1 oz. Marie Brizard Aphrodisiac
1 oz. amaretto
1 oz. fresh squeezed orange juice
1/2 oz. sweet & sour mix

Obeah Princess

1 oz. Galliano
1 oz. Mount Gay rum
3/4 oz. green crème de menthe
1 oz. egg white

Garnish with a slice of orange.

Old San Juan Sipper

1 1/2 oz. Bacardi dark rum
1 oz. lemon or lime juice
1/2 oz. white crème de menthe
1/4 oz. grenadine

Old Tavern Float

1 oz. DeKuyper root beer schnapps
1 oz. Gilbey's vodka
4 oz. orange juice
2 large scoops orange sherbet

Olympics Cocktail

1 1/2 oz. Bacardi dark rum
3/4 oz. lemon or lime juice
1/2 oz. cherry brandy

Garnish with a lemon or lime peel.

Opal

1 oz. gin
1 tbs. Cointreau
1 oz. orange juice
few drops orange flower water

Orange Cadillac

1 oz. Galliano
3/4 oz. white crème de cacao
1/2 oz. orange juice
1 1/4 oz. cream

Joe Beaudry
Australia

Orange Daiquiri

2 oz. light rum
1/2 oz. triple sec
1 oz. orange juice
1/2 oz. lime juice

Orange Margarita

1 1/2 oz. Jose Cuervo gold tequila
1/2 oz. Cointreau
3 oz. orange juice
1/2 oz. sweet & sour mix

Garnish with a slice of orange.

Orange Matador

1 1/2 oz. tequila
1 oz. pineapple juice
1 oz. orange juice
1 tbs. lime juice

Orange Smoothie

1 oz. Cointreau
3 oz. Coco Lopez cream of coconut
3 oz. light cream

Orange Velvet

1/2 oz. California white port
1/2 oz. orange juice
1 tbs. lemon juice

Orange Vodka Delight

2 oz. Gordon's orange vodka
1 12-oz. can frozen orange juice
2 oz. orange-flavored water

Garnish with a slice of orange over the rim.

Organ Grinder

1/2 oz. dark rum
1/2 oz. light rum
1/4 oz. rye whiskey
1/4 oz. white crème de cacao
2 oz. Coco Lopez cream of coconut

Oriental Cocktail

1 1/2 oz. Bacardi light rum
3/4 oz. orange juice
1/2 oz. cherry brandy

Garnish with a maraschino cherry.

Out of Bounds

Equal parts:
   Kahlúa
   vodka
   butterscotch schnapps
   cream or milk

Garnish with a maraschino cherry.

Paddler's Passion

1 oz. Bacardi amber rum
1 oz. vodka
1 1/2 oz. passion fruit juice
1 1/2 oz. orange juice
dash coconut syrup
dash grenadine

Garnish with a pineapple and maraschino cherry.

Pamir Peach

1 oz. Stoli Persik vodka
1 oz. Disaronno amaretto
2 oz. orange juice
dash lemon juice

Pancho's Pleasure

1 oz. Irish cream liqueur
1/2 oz. almond liqueur
1/2 oz. hazelnut liqueur
1/2 oz. coffee liqueur
2 oz. Coco Lopez cream of coconut

Panda Bear

1 oz. amaretto
1 oz. dark crème de cacao
2 oz. vanilla ice cream

Garnish with a maraschino cherry.

Pantomime

3 oz. dry vermouth
3-5 dashes grenadine
3-5 dashes orgeat syrup
1 egg white

Paradise Cocktail

1 oz. apricot brandy
1 oz. gin
1 oz. orange juice

Parisian Blonde

1 1/2 oz. Bacardi light rum
3/4 oz. cream
1/2 oz. orange curacao

Garnish with a maraschino cherry.

Passion Alessandro

1 oz. Opal Nera
1 oz. Hiram Walker crème de cacao
1 oz. heavy cream

Garnish with a maraschino cherry.

Passionate Margarita

1 1/2 oz. Alizé
1 oz. tequila
1 oz. lime juice

Passoã Jungle Juice

2 oz. Passoã
1 oz. Galliano
3 oz. orange juice

Pavlova Peach

1 1/2 oz. Stoli Persik vodka
2 oz. cranberry juice
2 oz. orange juice
peach slice

Peach Alexander

1 oz. peach schnapps
1/2 oz. white crème de cacao
1/2 fresh or canned peach
3 oz. vanilla ice cream

Garnish with a maraschino cherry.

Peach Banana Daiquiri

1 1/2 oz. Puerto Rican light rum
1/2 oz. medium banana, diced
1 oz. fresh lime juice
1/4 cup sliced peaches (fresh, frozen, or canned)

Peach Daiquiri

1 oz. rum
1 oz. triple sec
1 oz. lime juice
1 tsp. sugar
1/2 peach, sliced

Peach Irish

1 1/2 oz. Irish whiskey
1 ripe peach (peeled, pitted, and sliced)
1/2 cup fresh lime juice
1 oz. apricot brandy
1 tbs. superfine sugar
dash vanilla extract

Peach Margarita

1 1/2 oz. tequila
1 oz. peach liqueur
1 tsp. triple sec
1 oz. lime juice or juice of 1/2 lime
salt and lime wedge to rim glass

Peach Melba

1/2 oz. Captain Morgan spiced rum
3/4 oz. raspberry liqueur
2 oz. peach cocktail mix
1 oz. heavy cream
2 peach halves

Top with raspberry syrup.

Peach Rumnog

2 oz. rum
1 tsp. lemon juice
1 tbs. sugar
1 egg
1 fresh peach, pitted, or canned peach halves

Peach Tree Cobbler

1 oz. DeKuyper Peachtree schnapps
1 oz. apple barrel schnapps

Peach Velvet

1 1/2 oz. peach schnapps
1/2 oz. white crème de cacao
1/2 oz. heavy cream

Garnish with a maraschino cherry.

Peaches 'N Cream

1 oz. peach schnapps
1 oz. rum
3 oz. Coco Lopez cream of coconut
1 oz. vanilla ice cream

Garnish with a maraschino cherry.

Peachy Orange Colada

1 1/2 oz. peach schnapps
2 oz. orange juice
2 oz. Coco Lopez cream of coconut
1/2 oz. grenadine

Garnish with a maraschino cherry.

Peanut Butter Cup

2 oz. Malibu rum
1 oz. Smirnoff vodka
2 tbs. creamy peanut butter
2 tbs. chocolate syrup
2 scoops vanilla ice cream

Peppermint Patty

1 oz. white crème de cacao
1 oz. peppermint schnapps
1 oz. cream

Peppermint Stinger

1 1/2 oz. brandy
1 oz. peppermint schnapps

Pernod Flip

2 oz. Pernod
1 1/2 oz. half-and-half
1/2 oz. orgeat syrup
1 egg

Sprinkle with nutmeg.

Piña Colada

1 1/2 oz. rum
1 oz. Coco Lopez cream of coconut
2 oz. pineapple juice

Piña Koalapear

2 oz. DeKuyper Harvest Pear schnapps
1 oz. CocoRibe coconut rum
1 oz. cream

Garnish with a maraschino cherry.

Piñata

1 1/2 oz. tequila
1/2 oz. banana liqueur
1 oz. lime juice

Pineapple Bomb Margarita

1 oz. Jose Cuervo tequila
1 oz. Grand Marnier
1/2 oz. vodka
3 oz. pineapple juice

Pineapple Burster

1/2 oz. light rum
1/2 oz. Marie Brizard pineapple-coconut
1/2 oz. pineapple juice

Pineapple Cooler

1/2 oz. Jamaican rum
1 oz. gin
1 oz. pineapple juice
2 oz. lime or lemon juice
2 tsp. sugar or grenadine

Pineapple Cooler II

1 oz. gin
2 slices fresh pineapple, cut in pieces
1/2 oz. green crème de menthe

Pineapple Daiquiri

1 1/2 oz. light rum
1/2 oz. triple sec
1 oz. Rose's lime juice
3 oz. pineapple juice

Pineapple Fusion

2 oz. Passoã
1/2 oz. tequila
3 oz. pineapple juice
2 oz. orange juice

Serve in a long drink glass full of ice. Garnish with a split pineapple wedge on the rim.

Pineapple Mist

2 oz. light rum
3 oz. pineapple juice

Pink Cloud

2 oz. gin
2 oz. pineapple juice
1 oz. grenadine
1 egg white

Pink Elephant

1 oz. Appleton dark rum
1 oz. Wray & Nephew overproof rum
3/4 oz. crème de banana
splash crème de noya
1/2 fresh banana
1 scoop vanilla ice cream

Garnish with a banana and maraschino cherry.

Pink Lady Number One

1 oz. gin
1 tbs. apple brandy
1 tbs. lemon juice
1 tbs. grenadine syrup
1 egg white

Pink Lady

1 1/2 oz. gin
1 1/2 oz. vanilla ice cream
1 tsp. grenadine

Pink Matador

1 1/2 oz. Sauza tequila
2 oz. pineapple juice
1/2 oz. lime juice
1/2 oz. grenadine

Pink Panther

1 1/4 oz. Sauza tequila
1/2 oz. grenadine
2 oz. cream or half-and-half

Pink Panther II

1 1/4 oz. Bacardi light rum
3/4 oz. lemon juice
3/4 oz. cream
1/2 oz. Rose's grenadine

Pink Velvet

1 oz. Hiram Walker chocolate cherry
1/2 oz. Hiram Walker crème de cassis
1 oz. cream

Pino Frio

2 oz. white rum
1 slice fresh pineapple
1 tbs. sugar

Pinsk Peach

1 1/2 oz. Stoli Persik vodka
3/4 oz. blue curacao
1/4 oz. diced pineapple, fresh or canned
dash lemon juice

Planter's Punch

1 1/2 oz. Jamaican rum
1 oz. orange juice
1 oz. pineapple juice
2 oz. lime or lemon juice
2 tsp. sugar or grenadine

Blend. Float Jamaican dark rum on top.

Platinum Blonde

1 1/2 oz. Bacardi light or dark rum
3/4 oz. cream
1/2 oz. triple sec

Plum Goofer

4 oz. Zinfandel
1–2 canned plums, seeded
2 oz. simple syrup
1/4 oz. red seedless grapes
1 cup ice cubes

Blend until smooth. Garnish with a plum slice and red grapes.

©2000 Vita-Mix Corporation

Poinciana

1 oz. light rum
2 maraschino cherries
1 oz. apple juice
1/2 oz. grenadine

Garnish with a sliced orange.

Polar Ice Cap

1 oz. vodka
1/2 oz. coffee liqueur
1 oz. Coco Lopez cream of coconut
1 oz. half-and-half

Polynesian Paradise

2 oz. Bacardi light or dark rum
2 oz. pineapple juice
1 oz. cream
1 oz. grenadine

Garnish with a pineapple spear and maraschino cherry.

Polynesian Powerhouse

2 oz. Bacardi light or dark rum
1/2 oz. Bacardi 151 rum
1/2 oz. apricot brandy
1 oz. pineapple juice
1 oz. lemon or lime juice
1 oz. orange juice
1/2 oz. grenadine
2 dashes Angostura bitters

Garnish with fresh fruit slices (pineapple, lemons and limes, oranges, etc.).

Pompier Daisy

1 oz. crème de cassis
1 1/2 oz. French vermouth

Blend and top with club soda.

Port and Sherry Cobbler

2 1/2 oz. sherry
1 oz. port wine
1/2 tsp. curacao

Porto Flip

4 oz. port wine
1 oz. cognac
1 oz. thick cream
2 tsp. bar sugar

Blend and float yellow Chartreuse.

Presidente

1 oz. Bacardi rum
1 oz. dry vermouth
1 tsp. grenadine

Prince Igor's Nightcap

1 oz. Stoli Kafya vodka
1 oz. Bombay Sapphire gin
1 oz. light cream

Garnish with a maraschino cherry.

Princess Alexandra

1 1/2 oz. Stoli Vanil vodka
1 oz. white crème de cacao
1 oz. cream or half-and-half
pinch grated nutmeg

Puente Roman

2 oz. Harveys Bristol cream
1 1/2 oz. orange juice
1/2 oz. brandy
1 1/2 oz. heavy cream
dash Hiram Walker orange curacao

Pump Room Alexander

3 oz. gin or brandy
3 oz. whipping cream
3 oz. crème de cacao
3 oz. crème de menthe

Garnish with a maraschino cherry.

Pushkin's Milk Shake

1 oz. Stoli Kafya vodka
1 oz. Stoli Ohranj vodka
1 cup cold milk or half-and-half
powdered cocoa

Racquet Ball Fizz

1 1/2 oz. Bacardi light rum
2 oz. grapefruit juice
1 egg white

Blend and top with club soda.

Raspberry Colada

1 1/2 oz. rum
1 1/2 oz. Chambord
2 oz. pineapple juice
1 oz. Coco Lopez cream of coconut

Raspberry Delight

3/4 oz. Drambuie
3/4 oz. Hiram Walker raspberry schnapps
1/2 oz. Tia Maria
1 scoop ice cream
fresh raspberries

Raspberry Frost

2 oz. light rum
1 oz. Chambord
2 oz. Coco Lopez cream of coconut
dash lime juice

Garnish with a maraschino cherry.

Raspberry Sweet Tart

1 oz. Chambord
1 oz. Angostura lime juice
1 oz. triple sec

Razberi Blow Pop

1/2 oz. Stoli Razberi vodka
1/3 oz. Chambord
1/2 oz. banana liqueur
1/2 oz. Peachtree schnapps
1/2 oz. milk
splash grenadine

Gina Geremia
Downtown Taverne
New Haven, CT

Razzberrita

1 1/4 oz. raspberry schnapps
3/4 oz. tequila
2 oz. lemon/lime juice

Razzsputin

1 1/2 oz. Stoli Razberi vodka
3 oz. cranberry juice
2 oz. grapefruit juice
1/8 oz. lime juice

Garnish with a lime slice.

Red Carpet

2 oz. white rum
4 oz. lime juice
2 oz. cranberry juice
2 tbs. sugar

Red Hot Mama

1 oz. Kahlúa
1 oz. Red Hot schnapps or 4 dashes Tabasco
3 oz. cream or milk

Garnish with a maraschino cherry.

Red Lion

1 oz. gin
1 oz. Grand Marnier
1 oz. orange juice
1 oz. lemon juice

Regal Fizz

2 oz. brandy
1 oz. Benedictine
juice of 1/2 lemon
1 tsp. bar sugar

Blend and fill with carbonated water or seltzer.

Reserve Mai-Tai

1 oz. Whaler's Rare Reserve dark rum
1 oz. Whaler's Great white rum
1 oz. orgeat
1 oz. passion fruit juice
3 oz. orange juice
1/2 oz. lime juice

Reunion

1/2 oz. Romana sambuca
1/2 oz. vodka
1/2 oz. strawberry liqueur
6 ripe strawberries
3 oz. orange juice

Rhett Butler

1 oz. Cointreau
1 oz. Southern Comfort
3/4 oz. Rose's lime juice

Rhum Barbancourt Freeze

1 oz. grapefruit juice
2 oz. orange juice
2 oz. Rhum Barbancourt
1 oz. triple sec
1/2 oz. lime juice
1/2 cup ice cubes

Garnish with an orange wedge and a maraschino cherry.

Ricki Martini

2 oz. Passoã
1 1/2 oz. Mount Gay rum
1/4 oz. lime juice

Ritabu

2 oz. Malibu rum
1/2 oz. triple sec
1/4 oz. fresh lime juice

Roasted Toasted Almond

1 oz. vodka
1 oz. Kahlúa
1 oz. amaretto
1 oz. cream

Roman Cow

2 oz. rum
1 oz. Romana sambuca
1 oz. lemon or lime juice
1 banana, overripe
1 egg

Ron's Special

2 oz. dark rum
2 oz. light rum
4 oz. Coco Lopez cream of coconut
3 pineapple slices with juice
1/2 medium banana
6 maraschino cherries with juice
2 scoops vanilla ice cream

Garnish with a maraschino cherry.

Root Beer

1/2 oz. brandy
1/2 oz. dark crème de cacao
1/4 oz. Galliano
2 oz. milk

Blend and add cola.

Root Beer Colada

2 oz. Hiram Walker Old Fashioned root
  beer schnapps
3 oz. Coco Lopez cream of coconut

Root Beer Float

2 oz. Hiram Walker Old Fashioned root
  beer schnapps
2 oz. milk or vanilla ice cream

Rooty Tooty

2 oz. DeKuyper root beer schnapps
4 oz. orange juice

Rose Cocktail

1 oz. gin
1/2 oz. apricot brandy
1/2 oz. French vermouth
2 tsp. grenadine
1 tsp. lemon juice

Rose in June

1 oz. Chambord
1 oz. gin
juice of 1 orange
juice of 2 limes (small)

Rose Petal

1 oz. cognac
1 oz. white crème de cacao
1 scoop raspberry sherbet

Rose's International

1 1/2 oz. Midori melon liqueur
3/4 oz. pistachio liqueur
3/4 oz. Rose's lime juice

Rosemary

1 oz. gin
1/2 oz. cherry brandy
1/2 oz. French vermouth

Rum Blossom

1 1/2 oz. Appleton rum
1/2 oz. lemon juice
1/2 oz. powdered sugar
1 1/2 oz. orange juice

Rum Cobbler

2 oz. Jamaican rum
1 tsp. Bacardi light rum
1 tsp. pineapple syrup

Rum Collins

2 oz. Puerto Rican rum
1 tsp. sugar
1/2 lemon, peeled

Rum Cow

1 tsp. Angostura bitters
2 oz. rum
1 cup milk or ice cream

Garnish with a maraschino cherry.

Rum Fizz

2 oz. Bacardi light rum
1 oz. lemon juice
1 tbs. sugar
1 egg white

Rum Pickup

2 oz. Puerto Rican rum
2 oz. milk

Blend and fill with carbonated water or soda.

Rum Rita

2 oz. Whaler's Great white rum
1 oz. Cointreau
1 oz. lime juice
3 oz. pineapple juice
1/2 oz. passion fruit syrup

Blend with ice until smooth. Rub lime wedge around rim of glass and dip in coarse sugar, garnish with a lime wedge, and enjoy a margarita— Hawaiian style.

Rum Runner

1 1/2 oz. Bacardi Black rum
1 oz. blackberry brandy
1 oz. banana liqueur
1/2 oz. grenadine
1/2 oz. lime juice

Rum Yum

1 oz. Baileys Irish cream
1 oz. Malibu rum
1 oz. cream or milk

Rumidori

1 1/2 oz. Puerto Rican rum
1 oz. Midori melon liqueur
3 oz. orange or pineapple juice

Russian Funk

3 dashes vodka
dash lime juice
1/2 tsp. sugar
sparkling water

Top with sparkling water.

Russian Sombrero

1 1/2 oz. Stoli Kafya vodka
1 oz. Baileys Irish cream
2 oz. light cream

Salt Pond

1 1/2 oz. Appleton white Jamaican rum
1/2 oz. triple sec
1 oz. lemon or lime juice

Sambuca Amore

1 oz. Hiram Walker sambuca
1 oz. Hiram Walker coffee brandy

Sambuca Colada

1 oz. Romana sambuca
2 oz. Coco Lopez cream of coconut
2 oz. pineapple juice
1 1/4 oz. ice

Sambuca Satin

1 1/2 oz. Hiram Walker sambuca
3 oz. vanilla ice cream

Garnish with a maraschino cherry.

San Juan Cocktail

1 1/2 oz. Bacardi light rum
1 oz. grapefruit juice
1/2 oz. lemon or lime juice
1/4 to 1/2 oz. Coco Lopez cream of coconut

Blend. Float 1/4 oz. Bacardi 151 rum.

San Juan Side Car

1 1/2 oz. Bacardi light rum
1 oz. lemon or lime juice
1/2 oz. white crème de menthe

Moisten the rim of a cocktail glass and dip in sugar. Garnish with a lime wheel.

San Juan Sling

1 1/2 oz. Puerto Rican rum
3/4 oz. cherry brandy
3 oz. sweetened lemon mix
1/2 oz. grenadine

Blend and float grenadine.

San Juan

2 oz. light rum
1 tbs. brandy
1 1/2 oz. grapefruit juice
1 tbs. Coco Lopez cream of coconut
1 tbs. fresh lime juice

Float brandy on top.

Santiago Julep

2 oz. Bacardi light rum
2 tsp. grenadine
1 lime, peeled
2 tbs. pineapple juice

Sarah Screamer

1 oz. dark rum
1/2 oz. sloe gin
1/2 oz. citrus vodka
1/2 oz. peach schnapps
3 oz. pineapple-orange juice

Saronnada

1 1/2 oz. Disaronno amaretto
1/2 oz. vodka
1 oz. Coco Lopez cream of coconut
2 oz. unsweetened pineapple juice

Saronno Fruit Whirl

1/2 cup canned apricot halves or crushed
pineapple
1 oz. Disaronno amaretto
1 cup orange or pineapple orange yogurt

Sauza La Bamba

3/4 oz. Sauza Conmemorativo tequila
3/4 oz. Frangelico
1 banana
1/2 oz. orange juice

Blend and top with 7-Up.

Scorpion

1 oz. light rum
1/2 oz. brandy
1/2 oz. gin
1 oz. sweet & sour mix
2 oz. orange juice
dash white crème de menthe
dash bitters

Blend. Float 1 oz. white wine and garnish with an orchid.

Scorpion II

2 oz. gold rum
1 oz. brandy
1/2 oz. orgeat syrup
1 1/2 oz. fresh lemon juice
1 1/2 oz. orange juice

Garnish with orange and lemon slices.

Scotch Smoothie

1 1/4 oz. scotch
1/2 oz. Baileys Irish cream
1/2 oz. almond liqueur
1 oz. Coco Lopez cream of coconut
2 scoops vanilla ice cream

Garnish with a maraschino cherry.

Sea Breeze Margarita

2 oz. Sauza Conmemorativo tequila
3 oz. grapefruit juice
1 oz. cranberry juice

Garnish with lime wedges.

Serendipity

1 1/2 oz. amaretto
2 oz. pineapple juice
1 1/2 oz. Coco Lopez cream of coconut

Garnish with a maraschino cherry.

Sex in the Blender

1 oz. Kahlúa
1/2 oz. amaretto
2 oz. cream or milk

Garnish with two maraschino cherries.

Shaken Cherry

1 oz. Captain Morgan
1/2 oz. wild cherry brandy

Blend with vanilla ice cream and 2 oz. maraschino cherry juice. Garnish with a spot of whipped cream and a maraschino cherry.

Mike Reailly
Waterbury, VT

Shamrock

1 oz. Irish whiskey
1/2 oz. dry vermouth
1/2 oz. green crème de menthe
1/2 oz. Irish cream

Shark Bite

2 oz. Myer's Original dark rum
3 oz. orange juice
1 oz. lemon juice
1 oz. grenadine

Sharky Highball

2 oz. applejack
1/2 oz. bourbon
1 tsp. lemon juice
1 tsp. sugar syrup

Blend and fill with carbonated water or soda.

Ship's Mate

1 oz. dark Jamaican rum
1/2 oz. white crème de cacao
1/2 oz. white crème de menthe
1/2 oz. sweet vermouth

Sidecar

1 oz. Rémy Martin
1/2 oz. Cointreau
1/2 oz. lime juice
1 egg white

Silhouette

1 oz. gin
4 oz. maraschino cherry juice
4 oz. pineapple juice
1 oz. lemon juice
2–3 mint leaves
3–4 pineapple chunks and maraschino cherries

Serve in a margarita glass. Decorate with a maraschino cherry and pineapple.

Ronny Hovanessia
Glendale, CA

Silk Stocking

2 oz. white tequila
1/2 oz. crème de cacao
3 1/2 oz. evaporated milk or 2 scoops vanilla ice
   cream
2 oz. grenadine

Blend and top with cinnamon.

Silver Fizz

1 1/2 oz. gin or rum
juice 1/2 lemon
1 tsp. sugar
1 egg white

Slalom

1 oz. Absolut vodka
1 oz. white crème de cacao
1 oz. Romana sambuca
1 tsp. heavy cream

Sloe Tequila

3/4 shot tequila
1/4 shot sloe gin
splash lime juice

Slow Boat

2 oz. Appleton gold Jamaican rum
2 oz. orange juice
2 oz. grapefruit juice
1/2 tsp. superfine sugar
dash Angostura bitters

Float rum. Garnish with a maraschino cherry.

Slow Gin Colada

1 oz. light rum
1/2 oz. gin
1/2 oz. sloe gin
1/2 oz. vodka
2 oz. Coco Lopez cream of coconut
3 oz. orange juice

Smooth as Silk

3/4 oz. Vandermint liqueur
3/4 oz. Irish cream
1/2 oz. Copa de Oro coffee liqueur

Smooth Operator

1 oz. Frangelico
1/2 oz. Kahlúa
1/2 oz. Baileys Irish cream
1/2 banana

Smooth Screw

1 oz. Tia Maria
1/2 oz. Jamaican rum
3 oz. pineapple juice

Float the rum.

Snow Cap Colada

1 oz. almond liqueur
1 oz. white crème de cacao
1/2 oz. brandy
2 oz. Coco Lopez cream of coconut
1 oz. cream

Snow Drop

1/2 oz. Galliano
1/2 oz. Cointreau
1/2 oz. vodka
1/2 oz. white crème de cacao
1 oz. light cream
dash egg white

Snow Job

2 parts DeKuyper Harvest Pear schnapps
1 part cream or half-and-half

Snowball Colada

1 oz. light rum
1 oz. peach schnapps
1 oz. Coco Lopez cream of coconut
4 oz. orange juice
1 oz. grenadine

Somosa Bay

1 oz. Absolut vodka
1/2 oz. Grand Marnier
2 oz. sweet & sour mix
1 oz. orange juice
1/4 oz. Angostura lime juice

Southern Alexander

1 1/2 oz. Southern Comfort
1 1/2 oz. crème de cacao
2 oz. half-and-half or 2 scoops vanilla ice cream

Southern Banana Daiquiri

3 oz. Southern Comfort
1 ripe banana, sliced
1 oz. sweetened lime juice

Southern Colada

1 1/2 oz. Southern Comfort
1 oz. cream of coconut
2 oz. pineapple juice

Southern Lady

1 1/2 oz. Bacardi light rum
1/2 oz. grenadine
1 egg white
4 oz. grapefruit juice

Southern Smoothie

1 oz. Southern Comfort
1 oz. Coco Lopez cream of coconut
2 oz. cranberry juice cocktail

Southern Stinger

1 oz. Southern Comfort
3 oz. white crème de menthe

Garnish with a lemon twist.

Southern Strawberry Daiquiri

1 1/2 oz. Southern Comfort
3 strawberries, frozen
2 oz. orange juice

Garnish with a strawberry.

Soviet Cocktail

1 1/2 oz. vodka
1/2 oz. dry vermouth
1/2 oz. dry sherry

Add a twist of lemon peel as garnish.

Spanish Sparkler

2 oz. madeira wine
2 oz. red sparkling wine
1/2 fresh orange, peeled and quartered
1/2 scoop rainbow sherbet
1 cup ice cubes

Blend until smooth. Pour in a glass and fill with ginger ale. Garnish with an orange slice and red grapes.

©2000 Vita-Mix Corporation

Spearmint Colada

1 1/2 oz. Hiram Walker spearmint schnapps
3 oz. Coco Lopez cream of coconut
3 oz. vanilla ice cream

Garnish with a maraschino cherry and an orange slice.

Special Sour

1 oz. Grand Marnier
1 oz. scotch or bourbon
1 oz. lemon juice

Spectacular Daiquiri

3/4 oz. Mandarine Napoleon
3/4 oz. light rum
1/2 oz. lime juice

Spellbound Shake

1 oz. Kahlúa
1 oz. crème de cacao
iced coffee

Float cream or milk and garnish with a mint sprig.

Spiced Piña Colada

1 oz. Bacardi spiced rum
3 oz. Coco Lopez piña colada mix

Spirited Coffee Lopez

1 oz. Coco Lopez cream of coconut
6 oz. hot coffee
1/2 oz. Irish whiskey

Garnish with whipped cream and a maraschino cherry.

Splendito

2 oz. light rum
1/2 oz. Cointreau
3 pineapple chunks
1 tsp. sugar

Garnish with a maraschino cherry and a minted pineapple chunk.

Spyglass

1 oz. Captain Morgan spiced rum
2 scoops vanilla ice cream
1 tbs. honey
dash milk

St. Patrick's Day Special

1 1/2 oz. Bacardi light rum
1/2 oz. green crème de menthe
3/4 oz. lemon or lime juice

St. Petersburg Sundae

1 1/2 oz. Stoli Vanil vodka
1/2 oz. Disaronno amaretto
1 large scoop chocolate ice cream
toasted almonds, chopped

Standard Flip

2 oz. liquor or wine of your choice
1 whole egg
1 tsp. powdered sugar

Stinger

2 oz. brandy or cognac
1/2 oz. white crème de menthe

Stralmond Colada

1 oz. light rum
1 oz. almond liqueur
2 oz. Coco Lopez cream of coconut
3 oz. pineapple juice
1/2 cup sliced fresh strawberries
6 maraschino cherries with juice

Stranded South of France

1 oz. Chambord
2 oz. Bartenders Original strawberry tequila cream
2 scoops vanilla ice cream

Straw Hat

1 1/2 oz. Puerto Rican rum
1/2 oz. dark crème de cacao
1 1/2 oz. sweetened lemon mix

Strawberry Banana Colada

1 1/2 oz. rum
1/2 medium banana
2 oz. strawberries
2 oz. Coco Lopez cream of coconut

Strawberry Blonde

1 oz. Jose Cuervo tequila
1/2 oz. Grand Marnier
1/2 oz. Finlandia vodka
1/2 oz. pineapple juice
3 oz. strawberries, fresh or frozen

Strawberry Blonde II

1 oz. Stoli Strasberi vodka
1 oz. white crème de cacao
1/2 cup fresh or frozen strawberries
2 oz. vanilla ice cream

Strawberry Colada

2 oz. rum
1 oz. Coco Lopez cream of coconut
1/2 cup strawberries, fresh or frozen
4 oz. pineapple juice

Strawberry Colada II

1 1/4 oz. Leroux strawberry liqueur
1 oz. Coco Lopez cream of coconut
2 oz. pineapple juice

Strawberry Daiquiri

1 oz. Bacardi light rum
3 oz. Coco Lopez strawberry daiquiri mix

Strawberry Daiquiri II

1 can Bacardi tropical fruit mixer—
    strawberry daiquiri mix
3 oz. Bacardi Silver rum

Makes three 8 oz. drinks.

Strawberry Daiquiri Alizé

2 oz. Alizé
1/2 cup crushed ice
1/2 cup frozen strawberries
1 tbs. freshly squeezed lemon juice
1 tbs. superfine sugar

Strawberry Daiquiribe

2 oz. CocoRibe
1/2 cup fresh strawberries
1/2 oz. lime juice
1/2 tsp. superfine sugar

Strawberry Margarita

1 oz. tequila
1 oz. Rose's lime juice
1/2 oz. Cointreau
1/2 cup strawberries, fresh or frozen

Strawberry Patch

1 1/2 oz. Southern Comfort
3 oz. frozen strawberries
2 oz. orange juice

Strawberry Rose

4 oz. rose wine
1/2 cup strawberries, fresh or frozen
1/2 oz. Rose's lime juice
1 tbs. sugar

Strawberry Shake

1 1/2 oz. Disaronno amaretto
1/2 cup frozen, slightly thawed strawberries
1 scoop vanilla ice cream
1/2 cup milk

Summer Breeze

1 1/2 oz. Cruzan premium dark rum
2 oz. Coco Lopez cream of coconut
1 1/2 oz. orange juice
1 1/2 oz. pineapple juice

Summer Delight

1 1/2 oz. Bacardi light rum
3/4 oz. lemon or lime juice
1/2 tsp. sugar
dash bitters

Summer Sky Appleton V/X Orange Daiquiri

1 oz. Appleton Estate V/X Jamaican rum
juice of 1 orange
juice of 1/4 lime
1 tsp. sugar

Garnish with a sprig of mint and an orange rind.

Summer Squall

3/4 oz. dark rum
1/2 oz. Captain Morgan coconut rum
3 oz. grapefruit juice
3 oz. cranberry cocktail
1/4 oz. Rose's sweetened lime juice
1 1/2 cups ice

Pour into a 16 oz. glass. Garnish with a lime wedge.

Sunshine Colada

3/4 oz. brandy
1/2 oz. Grand Marnier
1 oz. Coco Lopez
1 1/2 oz. orange juice
1/2 oz. cream
1 cup ice

Sunshine Frosty Punch

1 1/4 oz. vodka
2 scoops vanilla ice cream

Garnish with a maraschino cherry.

Sunshine Surprise

2 oz. white Riesling
1 banana, reserve some for garnish
2 oz. Coco Lopez cream of coconut
2 oz. simple syrup
1 cup ice cubes

Blend until smooth. Garnish with a banana flag.

©2000 Vita-Mix Corporation

Sunsplash

1 1/4 oz. Frangelico
3/4 oz. Captain Morgan spiced rum
3/4 oz. Coco Lopez cream of coconut
5 oz. orange juice

Surf's Up

1 oz. rum
1/2 oz. crème de banana
1/2 oz. crème de cacao
5 oz. pineapple juice
1 oz. cream

Garnish with three maraschino cherries.

Susquehanna Sunrise

1 1/2 oz. wilderberry schnapps
3 oz. cranberry juice
1 oz. orange juice
1 oz. grapefruit juice
1 oz. maraschino cherry juice
1 oz. strawberry daiquiri mix

Luciano Miele
Williamsport, PA

Sweet Almond

1 1/2 oz. Disaronno amaretto
1/2 oz. rum
1 oz. Coco Lopez cream of coconut
1/2 oz. cream

Sweet Georgia Brown

2 oz. Southern Comfort
2 oz. coffee

Sweet Yello Gal

2 oz. Bacardi dark
2 oz. Coco Lopez cream of coconut
3 oz. frozen mango
1 oz. sweetened pineapple juice, frozen
1/2 oz. simple syrup

Taboo

1 oz. Finlandia vodka, chilled
1/2 oz. cranberry juice
1/2 oz. pineapple juice
1/2 oz. sweet & sour mix
splash triple sec

Garnish with a pineapple wedge and a maraschino cherry.

Tabuka

2 oz. rum
1 tbs. sugar
1/4 fresh apple, peeled & cored
1 tbs. lemon juice

Tahoe Cocktail

1 1/2 oz. Bacardi light rum
1/2 oz. cherry liqueur
3/4 oz. lemon or lime juice

Tall Tahoe

1 1/2 oz. Bacardi light rum
1/2 oz. light crème de cacao
1/2 oz. cherry brandy cream

Garnish with a maraschino cherry.

Tamara Lvova

1 oz. Stoli Strasberi vodka
1 oz. Rhum Barbancourt
1 oz. crème de cacao
1 scoop vanilla ice cream

Top with whipped cream and a maraschino cherry.

Tampa Bay Special

1 1/2 oz. Bacardi light rum
1/2 oz. light crème de cacao
3/4 oz. orange juice

Tashkent Cooler

1 1/2 oz. Stoli Persik vodka
1/2 oz. sloe gin
3 oz. freshly squeezed orange juice
orange slice

Tendryfury

1 oz. Baja Rosa liqueur
1 oz. Disaronno amaretto
milk or cream
5-6 maraschino cherries or 1 oz. maraschino
   cherry juice

Craig Brotherson
Salt Lake City, UT

Tennis Love Fizz

1 1/2 oz. Bacardi light rum
2 oz. orange juice
1 egg white

Blend and top with club soda.

Tequila Colada

1 oz. tequila
2 1/2 oz. Coco Lopez cream of coconut

Tequila Gimlet

1 1/2 oz. tequila
1 1/2 oz. Rose's lime juice

Garnish with a lime wheel or green cherry.

Tequilada

2 oz. gold tequila
2 oz. cream of coconut
4 oz. pineapple juice
slice of fresh pineapple

Texas Sunday

1 1/2 oz. Bacardi light rum
1/2 oz. anisette
1/2 oz. grenadine
2 oz. cream

The 5:15 Cocktail

2 oz. curacao or triple sec
1 oz. French vermouth
4 oz. whipping cream

The Don Julio Silver Margarita

1 oz. Don Julio silver tequila
1 oz. Rose's lime juice
2/3 oz. orange liqueur

The Flapper

3/4 oz. Mandarine Napoleon
1/4 oz. triple sec

Fill with orange juice.

The Peg Leg

1 oz. Captain Morgan spiced rum
2 oz. cranberry cocktail
3 oz. apple juice
1/2 oz. Rose's sweetened lime juice

Pour into a 16 oz. glass. Garnish with a tall cinnamon stick.

Tia Banana Ria

2 oz. coffee liqueur
1 oz. vodka
2 oz. Coco Lopez cream of coconut
2 oz. half-and-half
1/2 banana

Tidal Wave

3/4 oz. vodka
3/4 oz. Southern Comfort
dash grenadine
2 oz. orange sherbet

Tidal Wave II

3/4 oz. Midori melon liqueur
1/4 oz. rum
1 oz. orange juice
2 oz. piña colada mix
2 oz. sweet & sour mix

Garnish with a maraschino cherry.

Tidbit

1 oz. gin
1 scoop vanilla ice cream
1–3 drops dry sherry

Garnish with a maraschino cherry.

Tiger Tail

2 oz. Pernod
1/4 tsp. Cointreau
4 oz. fresh orange juice

Garnish with a lime wedge.

Tijuana Margarita

1 1/2 oz. tequila
1 oz. Hiram Walker Orchard orange schnapps
1 1/2 oz. sweet & sour mix

To Die For

1 oz. Godiva liqueur
1/4 oz. Licor 43
1/2 oz. cherry juice
1/2 oz. cream

*Pour into a cocktail glass with ice or strain into a
martini glass. Sprinkle with nutmeg and add a
cherry garnish.*

Rosetta Warren
Lodi, NJ

To Russia with Love

1 1/2 oz. Stoli Vanil vodka
1/2 oz. maraschino liqueur
1/2 oz. Coco Lopez cream of coconut
1 oz. cream or half-and-half
1 egg white (for two drinks)

Garnish with a maraschino cherry.

Toasted Almond

1 1/2 oz. Lazzaroni amaretto
1 oz. Copa de Oro coffee liqueur
2 oz. light cream

Toasty Almond Colada

1 oz. Coco Lopez cream of coconut
2 oz. cream
1 oz. almond liqueur
1 oz. Kahlúa

Tom Collins Freeze

1 1/4 oz. gin
3 oz. sweet & sour mix

Blend with ice until smooth. Garnish with an orange flag.

©2000 Vita-Mix Corporation

Top Banana

1 1/2 oz. Hiram Walker amaretto
1 oz. Hiram Walker crème de banana
2 oz. milk or cream

Garnish with a maraschino cherry.

Top Ten

1 1/4 oz. Captain Morgan spiced rum
1 oz. heavy cream
1 oz. Coco Lopez cream of coconut

Trade Winds

2 oz. gold rum
1/2 oz. Chambord
1/2 oz. lime juice
2 tsp. sugar syrup

Trail Mix

1/2 oz. Peachtree schnapps
1/2 oz. Disaronno amaretto
1/2 oz. Chambord
1/2 oz. Frangelico
1/2 oz. cherry juice

Blend with 6 oz. ice cream and top with whipped cream and a maraschino cherry.

Janet Bogart
Monmouth, IL

Tricolor Cocktail

1 oz. Licor 43
1 oz. melon liqueur
3 oz. Coco Lopez cream of coconut
2 oz. orange juice
1 slice kiwi fruit, peeled
dash grenadine
1 cup ice

Mix in a blender until smooth.

Triple Cherry Smash

1 oz. cherry brandy
1 oz. cherry pucker
3 maraschino cherries

Garnish with three cherries cut to fit on the rim of the martini glass.

Steven J. Scalsky
Alexandria, VA

Troika

1 oz. Stoli Persik vodka
1 oz. Disaronno amaretto
1/2 oz. sloe gin
1/2 oz. lemon juice

Tropica Cocktail

1 1/4 oz. Myers's rum
5 oz. pineapple juice
2 oz. grapefruit juice
dash grenadine

Garnish with a fresh orchid flower and a pineapple wedge.

Tropical Belle

1/2 oz. Galliano
1/2 oz. Calvados
1/2 oz. gin
1 barspoon maraschino cherry juice

Garnish with red and green cherries and serve with straws.

Tropical Blush

1 oz. vodka
1 oz. Coco Lopez cream of coconut
3 oz. cranberry juice cocktail

Tropical Breeze

1 oz. rum
1/2 oz. crème de banana
1 oz. Coco Lopez cream of coconut
2 oz. orange juice

Garnish with a pineapple spear and a maraschino cherry.

Tropical Cream Punch

1 1/2 oz. light rum
2 oz. Coco Lopez cream of coconut
3 oz. orange juice
2 oz. pineapple juice
1 oz. grenadine

Garnish with a maraschino cherry.

Tropical Freeze

1 1/4 oz. rum
1 oz. Coco Lopez cream of coconut
1 1/2 oz. orange juice
1 1/2 oz. pineapple juice
1 1/4 oz. rum
1/2 oz. grenadine

Garnish with a maraschino cherry.

Tropical Hut

2 oz. Midori melon liqueur
1 oz. rum
1 1/4 oz. sweet & sour mix
1/4 oz. orgeat syrup

Tropical Kahlúa

1 oz. Kahlúa
1/2 oz. vodka
3 oz. Coco Lopez cream of coconut

Tropical Paradise

1 1/4 oz. rum
2 oz. Coco Lopez cream of coconut
2 oz. orange juice
1/2 banana
1/4 oz. grenadine

Garnish with a maraschino cherry.

Tropical Passion

1 oz. Alizé
1 oz. Midori melon liqueur
3 oz. pineapple juice
1 oz. orange juice

Garnish with a speared pineapple wedge and maraschino cherry.

Tropical Peach

1 oz. banana liqueur
1 oz. peach schnapps
1 oz. Coco Lopez cream of coconut
2 oz. orange juice

Tropical Storm

1 shot dark rum
1/2 shot crème de banana
3 oz. orange juice
dash grenadine
1/2 ripe banana, sliced

Garnish with a maraschino cherry and an orange slice.

Tropical Treasure

1 1/4 oz. melon liqueur
1 oz. crème de banana
2 oz. Coco Lopez cream of coconut
2 oz. pineapple juice

Garnish with a maraschino cherry and an orange slice.

Tumbleweed

1 oz. Disaronno amaretto
1 oz. white crème de cacao
2 oz. cream

Garnish with a maraschino cherry.

Twist

3/4 oz. Absolut vodka
1/2 oz. Hiram Walker white crème de menthe
2 oz. orange sherbet

Vanil Cocktail

1 oz. Stoli Vanil vodka
1/2 oz. Bombay gin
1/2 oz. triple sec
2 oz. orange juice

Garnish with a maraschino cherry.

Vanilla Sunrise

1 oz. Whaler's Vanille rum
4 oz. orange juice
1 oz. grenadine

Vanya's Strawberry Fizz

1 1/2 oz. Stoli Strasberi vodka
2 oz. cranberry juice
6 large strawberries

Velvet Hammer

1 oz. Cointreau
1 oz. Kahlúa
1 oz. cream

Vermillion Twister

3/4 oz. brandy
3/4 oz. French vermouth
3 dashes curacao
2 drops Angostura bitters
1/4 oz. grenadine

Very Berry Colada

1 1/2 oz. wildberry schnapps
3 oz. Coco Lopez cream of coconut
2 oz. pineapple juice

Garnish with a maraschino cherry.

Very Cherry Berry

1 1/2 oz. Absolut vodka
1/2 oz. Chambord
1/2 oz. maraschino cherry juice
4 maraschino cherries

Frank Disciascio
Somers Point, NJ

Villa Roma

1 oz. Galliano
4 oz. orange juice
1/4 lime, squeezed

J. Gannon
Villa Roma
San Francisco, CA

Vodka Collins Freeze

1 1/4 oz. vodka
3 oz. sweet & sour mix

Garnish with an orange flag.

©2000 Vita-Mix Corporation

Vodka Margarita

1 1/2 oz. vodka
1 1/2 oz. sweet & sour mix
3/4 oz. lime juice
3/4 oz. Cointreau

Vodka Stone Sour

1 1/2 oz. Gordon's citrus vodka
1 tsp. lemon bar mix
2 oz. orange juice

Garnish with an orange slice and a maraschino cherry.

Volcano

1 oz. vodka
1/2 oz. crème de almond
2 oz. Coco Lopez cream of coconut
1 scoop vanilla ice cream

Garnish with a maraschino cherry.

Volga Cooler

1 oz. Stoli Vanil vodka
1 oz. crème de banana
1/2 oz. triple sec
lemon-lime soda

Garnish with a maraschino cherry.

Wallbanger Freeze

1 1/2 oz. vodka
3 oz. orange juice

Blend and top with 1/4 oz. Galliano.

Walley's Highball

1/2 oz. Cointreau
1/2 oz. crème de menthe
2 oz. gin
juice of 1/2 lemon

Blend and fill with carbonated water or soda.

Wango Tango

1 1/2 oz. Midori melon liqueur
3/4 oz. blue curacao
6 pineapple chunks
1–2 oz. heavy cream

Garnish with a maraschino cherry.

Watermelon Rum Runner

1/2 oz. dark rum
3/4 oz. light rum
1 oz. Marie Brizard watermelon liqueur
1/2 oz. Marie Brizard banana liqueur
1/2 oz. Marie Brizard blackberry liqueur
1 oz. grenadine

Wave Cutter

1 1/2 oz. Mount Gay rum
1 oz. orange juice
1 oz. cranberry juice

Wedding Belle

1 oz. cherry brandy
1 oz. gin
1 oz. Dubonnet
1 oz. orange juice

Whale's Breath

1 oz. Whaler's Pineapple Paradise rum
1 oz. cranberry juice
4 oz. orange juice

Whaler's Rum Rita

2 oz. Whaler's Great white rum
1 oz. triple sec
1 oz. lime juice
coarse salt
lime wedge

Whaler's Vanilla Rita

2 oz. Whaler's Vanille rum
1 oz. triple sec
1 oz. orange juice
1/2 oz. lime juice
orange wedge

Whisper Cocktail

1/2 oz. whiskey
1/2 oz. French vermouth
1/2 oz. Italian vermouth

White Cap

1 1/2 oz. Southern Comfort
1 1/2 oz. crème de cacao
half-and-half

White Gorilla

2 oz. DeKuyper root beer schnapps
1 1/2 oz. Gilbey's vodka
1/2 oz. milk

White Lily

2 oz. gin
1 1/2 oz. triple sec
1 1/2 oz. light rum
1/4 tsp. Pernod

White Mink

2 oz. Galliano
1 oz. Rémy Martin cognac
1 oz. white crème de cacao
1 scoop vanilla ice cream

White Plush Highball

1 1/2 oz. gin
1 oz. maraschino liqueur
4 oz. milk

White Russian

1 1/2 oz. vodka
1/2 oz. Kahlúa
1/2 oz. vanilla ice cream

White Tiger

1 oz. Tuaca
1/2 oz. white crème de cacao
3 oz. vanilla ice cream

Garnish with a maraschino cherry.

White Velvet

1 1/2 oz. Romana sambuca
1 egg white
1 oz. lemon juice

Who's Your Daddy

1 oz. Captain Morgan
1 1/2 oz. Bartenders Hot Sex
2 oz. Dad's root beer

Tim Lowery, WI

Wildberry Angel

2 shots Gordon's wildberry vodka
1 shot crème de cassis
1 12-oz. can frozen pink lemonade
2 cups strawberry-flavored water

Place a whole strawberry over the glass rim and serve.

Willawa

1 oz. Galliano
1/2 oz. Rémy Martin cognac
1/2 oz. cherry brandy
2 oz. cream

Dust with nutmeg.

Winter Frost

1 oz. brandy
1/2 oz. white crème de cacao
1/2 oz. white crème de menthe
3 oz. vanilla ice cream

Garnish with a maraschino cherry.

Winter in the Emerald Isle

1 oz. green crème de menthe
1 oz. Irish whiskey
3 oz. vanilla ice cream

Winter Orange Blossom

1 oz. gin
3 oz. orange juice
1/2 tsp. sugar

Wynbreezer

1 oz. dark rum
1 oz. triple sec
1 oz. Angostura lime juice
2 oz. orange juice

Yacht Club Fizz

1 1/2 oz. Bacardi light rum
2 oz. pineapple juice
1 egg white

Blend and top with club soda. Garnish with a pineapple spear and a maraschino cherry.

Zombie

2 1/2 oz. light rum
1 oz. dark rum
1 oz. triple sec
1/2 oz. apricot brandy
1 oz. unsweetened pineapple juice
1/2 oz. Angostura grenadine
1 oz. orange juice

Nonalcoholic Blender Drinks

Apple Berry Jive

6 oz. apple juice
2 oz. raspberries, thawed
2 scoops vanilla ice cream

Combine all ingredients in a blender until smooth and pour into a 16 oz. glass. Garnish with an apple slice.

Apple Strawberry Surprise

1 cup frozen strawberries, thawed
2 1/2 cups apple Juice
1/2 tsp. sugar
1 2-liter bottle Canada Dry ginger ale, chilled
fresh strawberries

Blend berries, apple juice, and sugar until smooth. Pour into glasses, filling each glass half full. Fill the remainder of each glass with chilled Canada Dry ginger ale. Garnish with a fresh strawberry. Makes four servings.

Appleberry Freeze

5 oz. apple juice
1 oz. strawberries in syrup

Combine all ingredients in a blender until smooth and pour into a 12 oz. glass. Garnish with a fresh strawberry.

Banana Lopez

2 oz. Coco Lopez cream of coconut
1 medium banana
1 tsp. lemon juice

Banana Smoothie

1 ripe banana cut into pieces
1 cup yogurt, plain or flavored
2 tbs. honey, or to taste, if desired
1/2 tsp. vanilla

Berry Surprise

1 cup frozen raspberries, thawed
1/2 tsp. sugar
2 1/2 cups apple juice
1 2-liter bottle Canada Dry ginger ale, chilled
fresh raspberries

Blend frozen berries, sugar, and apple juice until smooth. Fill glasses half full with mixture and add Canada Dry ginger ale to fill. Garnish with fresh raspberries. Makes four servings.

Bite of the Apple

5 oz. apple juice
1 oz. fresh lime juice
1 tbs. unsweetened applesauce

Garnish with ground cinnamon.

Blushing Bride

1 oz. Coco Lopez cream of coconut
4 oz. orange juice
3 oz. pink grapefruit juice
1/2 oz. grenadine

Blue Fruit Ice

5 oz. grapefruit juice
1 oz. blueberries, thawed
1/2 oz. Rose's grenadine syrup

Blueberry Shake

1/2 cup fresh blueberries
1 tbs. sugar
1 cup milk

Garnish with fresh blueberries. Fresh strawberries may also be used.

Bodacious Freeze

6 oz. cranberry cocktail
1/2 can peaches in heavy syrup
1/4 oz. Rose's grenadine syrup

Combine all ingredients in a blender until smooth and pour into a 16 oz. glass. Garnish with a lemon wheel.

Chiquitita

1 banana
2 oz. pineapple juice
1 oz. light cream
1 oz. grenadine

Blend for thirty seconds. Pour and serve. Garnish with an orange slice or paper umbrella.

Chocolate Banana Colada Shake

1/3 cup Coco Lopez cream of coconut
1/2 cup milk
1 tbs. chocolate syrup
1 1/2 cups chocolate or vanilla ice cream
1/2 cup sliced bananas

Chocolate Colada Shake

1/3 cup Coco Lopez cream of coconut
1/2 cup milk
1 tbs. chocolate syrup
1/2 cup chocolate or vanilla ice cream

Garnish with a maraschino cherry.

Chocolate Malted Milk

2 oz. syrup
1 scoop ice cream
1/2 pint milk
1 tsp. powdered, unflavored malt

Blend on high speed for about 1 1/2 minutes, or until mixture is thick and there is about twice the original amount. Serve in two soda glasses.

Clown Noses

3 oz. orange juice
1/3 cup maraschino cherries, stemless
splash Rose's grenadine syrup

Combine the juice and ice in a blender until smooth. Add the cherries and blend very briefly (large chunks of cherry should be visible). Top with grenadine and garnish with an orange wheel.

Coco Lopez Shake

2 1/2 oz. Coco Lopez cream of coconut
1 scoop vanilla ice cream

Garnish with a maraschino cherry.

Coco Mocha Lopez

4 oz. Coco Lopez cream of coconut
2 oz. cold, black coffee
1/2 tsp. brandy

Sprinkle with nutmeg.

Coconut/Cranberry Smoothie

3 oz. Angostura lime juice
8 oz. cranberry juice
3 oz. Coco Lopez cream of coconut

Crananna Chill

6 oz. cranberry cocktail
1/2 fresh banana
squeeze lemon wedge

Combine all ingredients in a blender until smooth and pour into a 16 oz. glass. Garnish with a lemon wedge.

Cranapple Slush

2 oz. cranberry cocktail
3 oz. apple juice
1 oz. Mr & Mrs T sweet & sour mix
1/2 oz. Rose's grenadine

Pour into a 16 oz. glass. Garnish with a lemon wheel.

Cranberry Cappuccino

7 oz. cranberry cocktail
3/4 oz. cold espresso
1/2 oz. hazelnut syrup
1 oz. half-and-half
pinch ground cinnamon

Combine all ingredients in a blender until smooth and pour into a 16 oz. glass. Garnish with ground cinnamon.

Cranberry Dew

6 oz. cranberry cocktail
2 oz. honeydew melon puree
1/4 oz. Rose's lime juice

Combine all ingredients in a blender until smooth and pour into a 16 oz. glass. Garnish with a lime wheel.

Cranberry Mint Freeze

6 oz. cranberry cocktail
3 After Eight dark chocolate thin mints
1 scoop vanilla ice cream

Combine all ingredients in a blender until smooth and pour into a 16 oz. glass. Garnish with whipped cream and an After Eight dark chocolate thin mint.

Cranberry Smoothie

6 oz. cranberry cocktail
1/2 Granny Smith apple, seeded
3/4 oz. raspberry syrup

Combine all ingredients in a blender until smooth and pour into a 16 oz. glass. Garnish with an apple slice.

Deep Freeze

4 oz. apple juice
1 oz. peach nectar
1 oz. ginger ale or Sprite

Combine the apple juice and nectar over ice in a 10 oz. glass and top with soda. Garnish with a lemon wheel.

Dreamsicle

4 oz. orange juice
2 oz. half-and-half
3 oz. peach nectar
3/4 oz. almond syrup

Pour into a 16 oz. glass and top with whipped cream. Garnish with a peach slice.

Floribbean Freeze

3 oz. grapefruit juice
3 oz. cranberry cocktail
1 tsp. Coco Lopez cream of coconut
2 scoops vanilla ice cream

Pour into a 16 oz. glass and garnish with an orange wedge.

Florida Banana Lopez

2 oz. Coco Lopez cream of coconut
4 oz. orange juice
1 medium banana

Frozen Apricot Orange Lopez

2 oz. Coco Lopez cream of coconut
1 1/2 oz. orange juice
2 oz. apricot nectar

Frozen Citrus Mary

5 oz. orange juice
4 oz. tomato juice
1/4 oz. Rose's sweetened lime juice
1/2 tsp. prepared horseradish
6 drops Worcestershire sauce

Combine all ingredients in a blender until smooth, pour into a 16 oz. glass, and garnish with an orange wheel.

Frozen Cranberry Cappuccino

6 oz. cranberry cocktail
3/4 oz. cold espresso
1 scoop vanilla ice cream

Combine all ingredients in a blender until smooth and pour into a 16 oz. glass. Garnish with ground cinnamon.

Frozen Lime Soda

1 6-oz. can frozen limeade concentrate,
   slightly thawed
1 6-oz. can frozen pineapple juice, slightly
   thawed
1 6-oz. can cold water
3/4 cup Canada Dry club soda
lime slices and maraschino cherries

*Garnish with a lime slice and maraschino cherry.
Makes six servings.*

Frozen Orange Mochaccino

5 oz. orange juice
1 tbs. chocolate syrup
1 oz. cold espresso

*Combine all ingredients in a blender until smooth
and pour into a 16 oz. glass. Garnish with an
orange wedge.*

Gin-Less Gimlet

juice of 1/2 lime
1 egg white
2 dashes Angostura bitters
2 tsp. sugar syrup (or to taste)

Grape Lopez

3 oz. Coco Lopez cream of coconut
4 oz. grape juice

Ground Pterodactyl Eyes

3 oz. grapefruit juice
3/4 oz. Mr & Mrs T piña colada mix
1/2 cup seedless red grapes

Combine the juice, colada mix, and ice in a blender until smooth. Add the grapes and blend briefly (leaving large chunks). Serve with a spoon.

Guacamole Cocktail

1 California avocado, diced
5 oz. tomato juice, chilled
2 oz. fresh lime juice, chilled
1 small green chile, chopped
1 garlic clove, minced
salt to taste
freshly ground black pepper to taste
lime wedge

Garnish with a lime wedge.

Jungle Punch

6 oz. apple juice
1 oz. canned mandarin oranges
1/2 banana

Combine all ingredients in a blender until smooth and pour into a 16 oz. glass. Garnish with an orange wedge.

Note: 1 oz. of orange juice can be substituted for the mandarin oranges.

Lime Sorbet Lopez

2 1/2 oz. Coco Lopez cream of coconut
1/2 oz. Major Peters' lime juice
1 scoop lime sherbet

Major Peters' Frozen Virgin Mary

4 oz. Major Peters' bloody mary mix
  (regular or hot & spicy)
5 oz. orange juice
1/4 oz. Major Peters' lime juice

Maui Squeeze

6 oz. orange juice
1/4 cup canned pineapple cubes (packed in juice)
1/2 oz. Mr & Mrs T piña colada mix

*Combine all ingredients in a blender until smooth
and pour into a 16 oz. glass. Garnish with an
orange or pineapple wedge.*

Melon Medley

4 oz. fresh orange juice
4 oz. cantaloupe, cubed
1/2 oz. fresh lemon juice

Mocho Joe Cooler

4 oz. brewed coffee
4 oz. evaporated milk or half-and-half
4 oz. mocha powder
whipped cream

Garnish with a maraschino cherry.

Mocquiri

3 oz. pineapple juice
1/2 tsp. Rose's lime juice
1/2 tsp. lemon juice
1 tsp. confectioner's sugar

Blend for twenty-five seconds. Serve garnished with a lime slice.

For a Mockardi, or mock Bacardi, add 1/2 oz. grenadine before blending.

Monterey Madness

6 oz. grapefruit juice
3 oz. cantaloupe puree
1/4 oz. Rose's lime juice

Garnish with a lime wedge. Note: Add a packet of sugar.

Morning

3 oz. tomato juice
1 egg
1/2 tsp. horseradish
1/2 tsp. lemon juice

Blend for thirty seconds. Sprinkle with celery salt.

Mountain Dew

6 oz. apple juice
3 oz. honeydew melon puree
squeeze lemon wedge

Garnish with a lemon wheel.

Nada Colada

1 oz. Coco Lopez cream of coconut
2 oz. pineapple juice

New Orleans Day

2 oz. Coco Lopez cream of coconut
1 oz. butterscotch topping
1 oz. half-and-half

Nor'easter Surprise

5 oz. grapefruit juice
2 oz. tomato juice
1/2 oz. Rose's sweetened lime juice

*Combine all ingredients in a blender until smooth
and pour into a 16 oz. glass. Garnish with a lime
wedge.*

Orange Fiesta

1/2 cup orange juice, chilled
1/4 cup vanilla ice cream
1/4 cup orange sherbet

Garnish with an orange slice and mint.

Orange Dream Milkshake

8 oz. orange juice
4 oz. milk
6 scoops vanilla ice cream
whipped cream (garnish)

Garnish with a maraschino cherry.

Orange Smoothie

2 1/2 oz. Coco Lopez cream of coconut
3 oz. orange juice
1 scoop vanilla ice cream

Sprinkle with nutmeg.

Orange Sorbet Lopez

2 oz. Coco Lopez cream of coconut
1 oz. orange juice
1 scoop orange sherbet

Orchard Freeze

5 oz. orange juice
1/2 Granny Smith apple, seeded
1/4 oz. Rose's sweetened lime juice

Combine all ingredients in a blender until smooth and pour into a 16 oz. glass. Garnish with an orange wedge.

Peach Blend

2 cups milk
2 cups ice
1 banana, sliced
2 14-oz. cans peaches
1 tsp. sugar
maraschino cherries

Combine the first five ingredients in a blender and blend until smooth. Serve immediately in a frosty mug. Garnish with a maraschino cherry. Makes two servings.

Peach Freeze

5 oz. orange juice
2 oz. peach nectar
3/4 oz. raspberry syrup

Combine all ingredients in a blender until smooth and pour into a 16 oz. glass. Garnish with a peach or orange slice.

Piña Colada Shake

1/2 cup pineapple juice, unsweetened
1/3 cup Coco Lopez cream of coconut

Pineapple Lopez

2 oz. Coco Lopez cream of coconut
1 1/2 oz. pineapple juice
1/2 banana

Pineapple Sorbet Lopez

1 1/2 oz. Coco Lopez cream of coconut
2 oz. pineapple juice
1 scoop pineapple sherbet

Pink Grapefruit Passion

5 oz. grapefruit juice
1/2 oz. Mr & Mrs T piña colada mix
2 oz. frozen raspberries

Pour into a 16 oz. glass. Garnish with a lime wedge.

Pink Sands

1 small can pineapple juice
1/2 tsp. sugar
2 tbs. cream
dash grenadine

Pour all ingredients over cracked ice in a tall glass. Stir.

Polynesian Pleasure

1 oz. pineapple juice
2 oz. orange juice
dash lemon juice

Rainbow Berry Smoothie

10 oz. apple/cranberry juice
4 oz. whole strawberries, frozen
2 oz. whole blackberries, frozen
2 scoops rainbow sherbet
1/2 banana

Raspberry Chill

1 cup fresh or frozen raspberries
1/2 cup nonalcoholic rose wine
1/2 cup sour cream
1 cup crushed ice
1 liter Canada Dry ginger ale
fresh raspberries

Combine first four ingredients in a blender and blend until smooth. Just before serving, add Canada Dry ginger ale and stir. Serve in chilled wine glasses with floating fresh raspberries for garnish. Makes eight servings.

Rose's Banana

1 oz. Rose's lime juice
1/2 large, ripe banana
1 tbs. confectioner's sugar

Serve garnished with a lime slice.

Strawberries and Cream Smoothie

4 oz. Mr & Mrs T strawberry daiquiri mix
4 scoops vanilla ice cream

Serve in a 10 oz. mug garnished with whipped cream.

Strawberry Banana Lopez

2 oz. Coco Lopez cream of coconut
2 oz. strawberries
1/2 medium banana

Strawberry Yogurt Punch

5 oz. orange juice
1 oz. strawberries in syrup
2 oz. vanilla yogurt

Combine all ingredients in a blender until smooth, pour into a 16 oz. glass, and garnish with a fresh strawberry.

Tangerine Squeeze

6 oz. orange juice
1/4 cup canned mandarin oranges
1/2 oz. Rose's grenadine syrup

Combine all ingredients in a blender until smooth and pour into a 16 oz. glass. Garnish with an orange or kiwi wedge.

The Apple Shadow

5 1/2 oz. apple juice
1/2 oz. Mr & Mrs T piña colada mix

Combine the apple juice and colada mix over ice in a 10 oz. glass and blend. Garnish with a lime wedge.

Tiger's Milk

3/4 cup plain yogurt
3/4 cup orange juice
1 banana, sliced
2 tsp. honey

Makes 2 servings.

Tropical Breeze

1/2 banana, sliced
1/2 cup milk
2 tbs. unsweetened pineapple juice
1 tsp. Coco Lopez cream of coconut

Tropical Freeze Lopez

2 oz. Coco Lopez cream of coconut
1 1/2 oz. orange juice
1 1/2 oz. pineapple juice

Wacky Jamaican Cabdriver

1 oz. orange juice
1 oz. Coco Lopez cream of coconut
1 oz. cranberry juice

Well Red Rhino

1 oz. cranberry juice cocktail
1 1/2 oz. strawberry daiquiri mix
1/2 oz. Coco Lopez cream of coconut
1 1/2 oz. club soda

Process cranberry juice, strawberry daiquiri mix, and Coco Lopez in a blender. Add club soda to the top and stir.

Worms and Dirt

5 oz. apple juice
1 Oreo chocolate sandwich cookie
1 scoop vanilla ice cream

Garnish with a gummy worm.